TEACHER'S PET PUBLICATIONS

PUZZLE PACK
for
The Picture of Dorian Gray

based on the book by
Oscar Wilde

Written by
Mary B. Collins

© 2008 Teacher's Pet Publications
All Rights Reserved

The materials in this packet are copyrighted
by Teacher's Pet Publications, Inc.

These pages may be duplicated by the purchaser
for use in the purchaser's own classroom.

Copying any of these materials and distributing them
for any other purpose is a violation of the copyright laws.

© 2008 Teacher's Pet Publications, Inc.
www.tpet.com

INTRODUCTION
If you already own the LitPlan for this title, this Puzzle Pack will refresh your Unit Resource Materials and Vocabulary Resource Materials sections plus give you additional materials you can substitute into the tests. If you do not already have a complete LitPlan, these pages will give you some supplemental materials to use with your own plan. There are two main groups of materials: one set for unit words (such as characters' names, symbols, places, etc.) and one set for vocabulary words associated with the book.

WORD LIST
There is a word list for both the unit words and the vocabulary words. These lists show you which words are being used in the materials and the clues or definitions being used for those words. You may want to give students a word list with clues/definitions to help them, or you may want students to only have a word list (without clues/definitions) if you want them to work a little harder. Both are available for duplication. The word lists can also be your "calling key" for the bingo games.

FILL IN THE BLANK AND MATCHING
There are 4 each of the fill in the blank and matching worksheets for both the unit and vocabulary words. These pages can be used either as extra worksheets for students or as objective parts of a unit test. They can be done individually if students need extra help or as a whole class activity to review the material covered.

MAGIC SQUARES
The magic squares not only reinforce the material covered but also work on reasoning and math skills. Many teachers have told us that their students really enjoy doing these!

WORD SEARCH PUZZLES
The word search words go in all directions, as indicated on your answer keys. Two of the word search puzzles have the clues listed rather than the words. This makes the puzzle a little more difficult, but it reinforces the material better. Two word search puzzles have words only for students who find the clue puzzles too difficult.

CROSSWORD PUZZLES
Both unit and vocabulary word sections have 4 crossword puzzles.

BINGO CARDS
There are 32 individual bingo cards for the unit words and 32 individual bingo cards for the vocabulary words. You can use your word list as a "call list," calling the words at random and marking them off of your list as you go, or you could use the flash cards by cutting them apart and drawing the words at random from a hat (or box or whatever). To make a better review, you might ask for the definition and spelling of each word as you call it out–or you could call out the definitions and have students tell you the words they need to look for on the puzzle.

JUGGLE LETTERS
The vocabulary juggle letter game is intended to help students learn the spellings of the words. One sheet has the definitions listed on it as an extra help for students who need it or to reinforce the definitions if you choose to do so.

FLASH CARDS
We've included a set of vocabulary flash cards you can duplicate, cut, and fold for your students. Some teachers make a few sets for general use by the class; others make a set for each student. Some teachers duplicate them for each student and have the students cut & fold their own. You can cut out just the words and put them in a hat, have each student pick out one word and write the definition and a sentence for that word. Students then swap words and papers, with the next student adding a sentence of his own under the last one. You can have students swap as many times as you like. Each time the student will read the sentences written prior to his own and then add a sentence. You can cut out the words and definitions separately and play "I Have; Who Has?" Each student in the room draws a word and definition. The first student says, "I have (the name of the word). Who has the definition?" The student with the definition reads it then says, "I have (the name of the vocabulary word she has). Who has the definition?" The round continues until all words and definitions have been given.

The Picture of Dorian Gray Word List

No.	Word	Clue/Definition
1.	BASIL	He painted the portrait of Dorian Gray.
2.	BEAUTY	Lord Henry tells Dorian the secret of life is the search for this.
3.	BERWICK	He leaves the smoking room when Dorian arrives.
4.	BOOK	It has a huge influence on Dorian's behavior.
5.	CAMPBELL	He disposes of Basil's body.
6.	CLOUSTON	He shoots the man hiding in the thicket.
7.	CORONER	Rules Sibyl's death a accident
8.	CRUELTY	The portrait showed this in the mouth.
9.	DORIAN	He murders Basil.
10.	DUCHESS	Person who asks Lord Henry how to become young again
11.	ERSKINE	He claims Lord Henry is extremely dangerous.
12.	FATHER	Dorian's was killed in a duel.
13.	GOOD	According to Lord Henry, to be this is to be in harmony with oneself.
14.	HARE	Dorian begs Sir Geoffrey not to shoot this.
15.	HENRY	He has a negative influence on Dorian: Lord ___.
16.	HETTY	Young peasant girl Dorian chooses to leave while she is still pure
17.	ISAACS	He advances Sibyl's family 50 pounds.
18.	JAMES	He wants to kill Dorian.
19.	JULIET	Sibyl's theater role
20.	LEAF	Dorian's housekeeper
21.	NARBOROUGH	She thinks living in the country is boring.
22.	OPERA	Dorian goes there after he learns of Sibyl's death.
23.	PARIS	Basil wants to exhibit Dorian's portrait there.
24.	PORTRAIT	Visual diary of Dorian's soul
25.	PRINCE	Sibyl knows Dorian by this 'Charming' name
26.	REALITY	It spoiled Sibyl's acting.
27.	RINGS	Dorian's servants can only identify his body by these.
28.	SATYR	Basil sees this in his portrait of Dorian.
29.	SHAME	Dorian chooses to allow the painting to bear the burden of his ___.
30.	SINGLETON	He sees Dorian at the opium house.
31.	SINS	Dorian believes that forgiveness for these is impossible.
32.	SOUL	Dorian claims this can be bought, sold, and bartered away.
33.	SPHINXES	Lord Henry describes women as these without secrets.
34.	SYBIL	She commits suicide.
35.	TELEGRAM	Dorian sends one to Lord Henry announcing his engagement.
36.	TEMPTATION	According to Lord Henry, the only way to get rid of this is to yeild to it.
37.	UGLY	Lord Henry says it is better to be good than this.
38.	UNSELFISH	Lord Henry says these people are colorless and lack individuality.
39.	VANE	Last name of Sibyl and James
40.	VICTORIA	Lord Henry's wife
41.	WAINSCOTING	Dorian hides Basil's belongings behind this.
42.	WILDE	Author
43.	YOUTH	The secret of this is to repeat the follies of it.

The Picture of Dorian Gray Fill In The Blanks 1

_____ 1. Sibyl's theater role

_____ 2. Dorian believes that forgiveness for these is impossible.

_____ 3. Dorian goes there after he learns of Sibyl's death.

_____ 4. According to Lord Henry, the only way to get rid of this is to yeild to it.

_____ 5. He has a negative influence on Dorian: Lord ___.

_____ 6. Dorian chooses to allow the painting to bear the burden of his ___.

_____ 7. Dorian hides Basil's belongings behind this.

_____ 8. Lord Henry's wife

_____ 9. She thinks living in the country is boring.

_____ 10. He wants to kill Dorian.

_____ 11. He sees Dorian at the opium house.

_____ 12. Dorian's housekeeper

_____ 13. He murders Basil.

_____ 14. He advances Sibyl's family 50 pounds.

_____ 15. Dorian begs Sir Geoffrey not to shoot this.

_____ 16. He painted the portrait of Dorian Gray.

_____ 17. Rules Sibyl's death a accident

_____ 18. Young peasant girl Dorian chooses to leave while she is still pure

_____ 19. Dorian sends one to Lord Henry announcing his engagement.

_____ 20. Lord Henry says it is better to be good than this.

The Picture of Dorian Gray Fill In The Blanks 1 Answer Key

JULIET	1. Sibyl's theater role
SINS	2. Dorian believes that forgiveness for these is impossible.
OPERA	3. Dorian goes there after he learns of Sibyl's death.
TEMPTATION	4. According to Lord Henry, the only way to get rid of this is to yeild to it.
HENRY	5. He has a negative influence on Dorian: Lord ___.
SHAME	6. Dorian chooses to allow the painting to bear the burden of his ___.
WAINSCOTING	7. Dorian hides Basil's belongings behind this.
VICTORIA	8. Lord Henry's wife
NARBOROUGH	9. She thinks living in the country is boring.
JAMES	10. He wants to kill Dorian.
SINGLETON	11. He sees Dorian at the opium house.
LEAF	12. Dorian's housekeeper
DORIAN	13. He murders Basil.
ISAACS	14. He advances Sibyl's family 50 pounds.
HARE	15. Dorian begs Sir Geoffrey not to shoot this.
BASIL	16. He painted the portrait of Dorian Gray.
CORONER	17. Rules Sibyl's death a accident
HETTY	18. Young peasant girl Dorian chooses to leave while she is still pure
TELEGRAM	19. Dorian sends one to Lord Henry announcing his engagement.
UGLY	20. Lord Henry says it is better to be good than this.

The Picture of Dorian Gray Fill In The Blanks 2

1. Dorian hides Basil's belongings behind this.
2. Basil wants to exhibit Dorian's portrait there.
3. Person who asks Lord Henry how to become young again
4. Basil sees this in his portrait of Dorian.
5. Dorian's housekeeper
6. He advances Sibyl's family 50 pounds.
7. He claims Lord Henry is extremely dangerous.
8. Lord Henry says it is better to be good than this.
9. He sees Dorian at the opium house.
10. The secret of this is to repeat the follies of it.
11. Dorian goes there after he learns of Sibyl's death.
12. Dorian's was killed in a duel.
13. Young peasant girl Dorian chooses to leave while she is still pure
14. Dorian believes that forgiveness for these is impossible.
15. He shoots the man hiding in the thicket.
16. Lord Henry tells Dorian the secret of life is the search for this.
17. It spoiled Sibyl's acting.
18. According to Lord Henry, to be this is to be in harmony with oneself.
19. Lord Henry describes women as these without secrets.
20. She thinks living in the country is boring.

The Picture of Dorian Gray Fill In The Blanks 2 Answer Key

WAINSCOTING	1. Dorian hides Basil's belongings behind this.
PARIS	2. Basil wants to exhibit Dorian's portrait there.
DUCHESS	3. Person who asks Lord Henry how to become young again
SATYR	4. Basil sees this in his portrait of Dorian.
LEAF	5. Dorian's housekeeper
ISAACS	6. He advances Sibyl's family 50 pounds.
ERSKINE	7. He claims Lord Henry is extremely dangerous.
UGLY	8. Lord Henry says it is better to be good than this.
SINGLETON	9. He sees Dorian at the opium house.
YOUTH	10. The secret of this is to repeat the follies of it.
OPERA	11. Dorian goes there after he learns of Sibyl's death.
FATHER	12. Dorian's was killed in a duel.
HETTY	13. Young peasant girl Dorian chooses to leave while she is still pure
SINS	14. Dorian believes that forgiveness for these is impossible.
CLOUSTON	15. He shoots the man hiding in the thicket.
BEAUTY	16. Lord Henry tells Dorian the secret of life is the search for this.
REALITY	17. It spoiled Sibyl's acting.
GOOD	18. According to Lord Henry, to be this is to be in harmony with oneself.
SPHINXES	19. Lord Henry describes women as these without secrets.
NARBOROUGH	20. She thinks living in the country is boring.

The Picture of Dorian Gray Fill In The Blanks 3

1. Dorian's housekeeper
2. Lord Henry says these people are colorless and lack individuality.
3. He sees Dorian at the opium house.
4. He shoots the man hiding in the thicket.
5. Basil sees this in his portrait of Dorian.
6. Young peasant girl Dorian chooses to leave while she is still pure
7. He murders Basil.
8. Dorian sends one to Lord Henry announcing his engagement.
9. According to Lord Henry, to be this is to be in harmony with oneself.
10. Dorian chooses to allow the painting to bear the burden of his ___.
11. Author
12. According to Lord Henry, the only way to get rid of this is to yeild to it.
13. Rules Sibyl's death a accident
14. Lord Henry's wife
15. It spoiled Sibyl's acting.
16. Lord Henry says it is better to be good than this.
17. She commits suicide.
18. Dorian goes there after he learns of Sibyl's death.
19. Last name of Sibyl and James
20. He claims Lord Henry is extremely dangerous.

The Picture of Dorian Gray Fill In The Blanks 3 Answer Key

LEAF	1. Dorian's housekeeper
UNSELFISH	2. Lord Henry says these people are colorless and lack individuality.
SINGLETON	3. He sees Dorian at the opium house.
CLOUSTON	4. He shoots the man hiding in the thicket.
SATYR	5. Basil sees this in his portrait of Dorian.
HETTY	6. Young peasant girl Dorian chooses to leave while she is still pure
DORIAN	7. He murders Basil.
TELEGRAM	8. Dorian sends one to Lord Henry announcing his engagement.
GOOD	9. According to Lord Henry, to be this is to be in harmony with oneself.
SHAME	10. Dorian chooses to allow the painting to bear the burden of his ___.
WILDE	11. Author
TEMPTATION	12. According to Lord Henry, the only way to get rid of this is to yeild to it.
CORONER	13. Rules Sibyl's death a accident
VICTORIA	14. Lord Henry's wife
REALITY	15. It spoiled Sibyl's acting.
UGLY	16. Lord Henry says it is better to be good than this.
SYBIL	17. She commits suicide.
OPERA	18. Dorian goes there after he learns of Sibyl's death.
VANE	19. Last name of Sibyl and James
ERSKINE	20. He claims Lord Henry is extremely dangerous.

The Picture of Dorian Gray Fill In The Blanks 4

_____ 1. Person who asks Lord Henry how to become young again

_____ 2. He painted the portrait of Dorian Gray.

_____ 3. Dorian begs Sir Geoffrey not to shoot this.

_____ 4. He murders Basil.

_____ 5. He sees Dorian at the opium house.

_____ 6. According to Lord Henry, the only way to get rid of this is to yeild to it.

_____ 7. Dorian hides Basil's belongings behind this.

_____ 8. Dorian chooses to allow the painting to bear the burden of his ___.

_____ 9. Dorian sends one to Lord Henry announcing his engagement.

_____ 10. Young peasant girl Dorian chooses to leave while she is still pure

_____ 11. The secret of this is to repeat the follies of it.

_____ 12. The portrait showed this in the mouth.

_____ 13. Sibyl's theater role

_____ 14. He advances Sibyl's family 50 pounds.

_____ 15. Lord Henry says these people are colorless and lack individuality.

_____ 16. Lord Henry describes women as these without secrets.

_____ 17. She commits suicide.

_____ 18. Basil sees this in his portrait of Dorian.

_____ 19. Sibyl knows Dorian by this 'Charming' name

_____ 20. It has a huge influence on Dorian's behavior.

The Picture of Dorian Gray Fill In The Blanks 4 Answer Key

DUCHESS	1. Person who asks Lord Henry how to become young again
BASIL	2. He painted the portrait of Dorian Gray.
HARE	3. Dorian begs Sir Geoffrey not to shoot this.
DORIAN	4. He murders Basil.
SINGLETON	5. He sees Dorian at the opium house.
TEMPTATION	6. According to Lord Henry, the only way to get rid of this is to yeild to it.
WAINSCOTING	7. Dorian hides Basil's belongings behind this.
SHAME	8. Dorian chooses to allow the painting to bear the burden of his ___.
TELEGRAM	9. Dorian sends one to Lord Henry announcing his engagement.
HETTY	10. Young peasant girl Dorian chooses to leave while she is still pure
YOUTH	11. The secret of this is to repeat the follies of it.
CRUELTY	12. The portrait showed this in the mouth.
JULIET	13. Sibyl's theater role
ISAACS	14. He advances Sibyl's family 50 pounds.
UNSELFISH	15. Lord Henry says these people are colorless and lack individuality.
SPHINXES	16. Lord Henry describes women as these without secrets.
SYBIL	17. She commits suicide.
SATYR	18. Basil sees this in his portrait of Dorian.
PRINCE	19. Sibyl knows Dorian by this 'Charming' name
BOOK	20. It has a huge influence on Dorian's behavior.

The Picture of Dorian Gray Matching 1

___ 1. REALITY
___ 2. TEMPTATION
___ 3. WILDE
___ 4. HARE
___ 5. CAMPBELL
___ 6. SOUL
___ 7. BERWICK
___ 8. HETTY
___ 9. LEAF
___ 10. JAMES
___ 11. HENRY
___ 12. ERSKINE
___ 13. SHAME
___ 14. SINS
___ 15. OPERA
___ 16. SPHINXES
___ 17. PORTRAIT
___ 18. BEAUTY
___ 19. PARIS
___ 20. BOOK
___ 21. YOUTH
___ 22. UNSELFISH
___ 23. PRINCE
___ 24. BASIL
___ 25. CRUELTY

A. Dorian begs Sir Geoffrey not to shoot this.
B. It spoiled Sibyl's acting.
C. He wants to kill Dorian.
D. Visual diary of Dorian's soul
E. Dorian goes there after he learns of Sibyl's death.
F. Sibyl knows Dorian by this 'Charming' name
G. Author
H. Lord Henry says these people are colorless and lack individuality.
I. Lord Henry tells Dorian the secret of life is the search for this.
J. Basil wants to exhibit Dorian's portrait there.
K. The portrait showed this in the mouth.
L. Lord Henry describes women as these without secrets.
M. He claims Lord Henry is extremely dangerous.
N. Dorian's housekeeper
O. He leaves the smoking room when Dorian arrives.
P. It has a huge influence on Dorian's behavior.
Q. Dorian claims this can be bought, sold, and bartered away.
R. According to Lord Henry, the only way to get rid of this is to yeild to it.
S. The secret of this is to repeat the follies of it.
T. He has a negative influence on Dorian: Lord ___.
U. He painted the portrait of Dorian Gray.
V. Dorian believes that forgiveness for these is impossible.
W. Dorian chooses to allow the painting to bear the burden of his ___.
X. Young peasant girl Dorian chooses to leave while she is still pure
Y. He disposes of Basil's body.

The Picture of Dorian Gray Matching 1 Answer Key

B - 1. REALITY	A.	Dorian begs Sir Geoffrey not to shoot this.
R - 2. TEMPTATION	B.	It spoiled Sibyl's acting.
G - 3. WILDE	C.	He wants to kill Dorian.
A - 4. HARE	D.	Visual diary of Dorian's soul
Y - 5. CAMPBELL	E.	Dorian goes there after he learns of Sibyl's death.
Q - 6. SOUL	F.	Sibyl knows Dorian by this 'Charming' name
O - 7. BERWICK	G.	Author
X - 8. HETTY	H.	Lord Henry says these people are colorless and lack individuality.
N - 9. LEAF	I.	Lord Henry tells Dorian the secret of life is the search for this.
C - 10. JAMES	J.	Basil wants to exhibit Dorian's portrait there.
T - 11. HENRY	K.	The portrait showed this in the mouth.
M - 12. ERSKINE	L.	Lord Henry describes women as these without secrets.
W - 13. SHAME	M.	He claims Lord Henry is extremely dangerous.
V - 14. SINS	N.	Dorian's housekeeper
E - 15. OPERA	O.	He leaves the smoking room when Dorian arrives.
L - 16. SPHINXES	P.	It has a huge influence on Dorian's behavior.
D - 17. PORTRAIT	Q.	Dorian claims this can be bought, sold, and bartered away.
I - 18. BEAUTY	R.	According to Lord Henry, the only way to get rid of this is to yeild to it.
J - 19. PARIS	S.	The secret of this is to repeat the follies of it.
P - 20. BOOK	T.	He has a negative influence on Dorian: Lord ___.
S - 21. YOUTH	U.	He painted the portrait of Dorian Gray.
H - 22. UNSELFISH	V.	Dorian believes that forgiveness for these is impossible.
F - 23. PRINCE	W.	Dorian chooses to allow the painting to bear the burden of his ___.
U - 24. BASIL	X.	Young peasant girl Dorian chooses to leave while she is still pure
K - 25. CRUELTY	Y.	He disposes of Basil's body.

The Picture of Dorian Gray Matching 2

___ 1. SINS
___ 2. HENRY
___ 3. JAMES
___ 4. BOOK
___ 5. YOUTH
___ 6. BASIL
___ 7. OPERA
___ 8. SPHINXES
___ 9. SHAME
___ 10. VANE
___ 11. CLOUSTON
___ 12. HARE
___ 13. SYBIL
___ 14. RINGS
___ 15. JULIET
___ 16. ISAACS
___ 17. SOUL
___ 18. UGLY
___ 19. WILDE
___ 20. FATHER
___ 21. TELEGRAM
___ 22. LEAF
___ 23. CAMPBELL
___ 24. CRUELTY
___ 25. REALITY

A. The secret of this is to repeat the follies of it.
B. He painted the portrait of Dorian Gray.
C. It spoiled Sibyl's acting.
D. Dorian's servants can only identify his body by these.
E. Dorian claims this can be bought, sold, and bartered away.
F. He advances Sibyl's family 50 pounds.
G. Lord Henry says it is better to be good than this.
H. He wants to kill Dorian.
I. He has a negative influence on Dorian: Lord ___.
J. Dorian begs Sir Geoffrey not to shoot this.
K. Lord Henry describes women as these without secrets.
L. She commits suicide.
M. Dorian's housekeeper
N. Dorian sends one to Lord Henry announcing his engagement.
O. Dorian goes there after he learns of Sibyl's death.
P. The portrait showed this in the mouth.
Q. It has a huge influence on Dorian's behavior.
R. Last name of Sibyl and James
S. Sibyl's theater role
T. Dorian believes that forgiveness for these is impossible.
U. He disposes of Basil's body.
V. He shoots the man hiding in the thicket.
W. Dorian's was killed in a duel.
X. Author
Y. Dorian chooses to allow the painting to bear the burden of his ___.

The Picture of Dorian Gray Matching 2 Answer Key

T - 1.	SINS	A. The secret of this is to repeat the follies of it.
I - 2.	HENRY	B. He painted the portrait of Dorian Gray.
H - 3.	JAMES	C. It spoiled Sibyl's acting.
Q - 4.	BOOK	D. Dorian's servants can only identify his body by these.
A - 5.	YOUTH	E. Dorian claims this can be bought, sold, and bartered away.
B - 6.	BASIL	F. He advances Sibyl's family 50 pounds.
O - 7.	OPERA	G. Lord Henry says it is better to be good than this.
K - 8.	SPHINXES	H. He wants to kill Dorian.
Y - 9.	SHAME	I. He has a negative influence on Dorian: Lord ___.
R -10.	VANE	J. Dorian begs Sir Geoffrey not to shoot this.
V -11.	CLOUSTON	K. Lord Henry describes women as these without secrets.
J -12.	HARE	L. She commits suicide.
L -13.	SYBIL	M. Dorian's housekeeper
D -14.	RINGS	N. Dorian sends one to Lord Henry announcing his engagement.
S -15.	JULIET	O. Dorian goes there after he learns of Sibyl's death.
F -16.	ISAACS	P. The portrait showed this in the mouth.
E -17.	SOUL	Q. It has a huge influence on Dorian's behavior.
G -18.	UGLY	R. Last name of Sibyl and James
X -19.	WILDE	S. Sibyl's theater role
W -20.	FATHER	T. Dorian believes that forgiveness for these is impossible.
N -21.	TELEGRAM	U. He disposes of Basil's body.
M -22.	LEAF	V. He shoots the man hiding in the thicket.
U -23.	CAMPBELL	W. Dorian's was killed in a duel.
P -24.	CRUELTY	X. Author
C -25.	REALITY	Y. Dorian chooses to allow the painting to bear the burden of his ___.

The Picture of Dorian Gray Matching 3

___ 1. DUCHESS
___ 2. CRUELTY
___ 3. CORONER
___ 4. TEMPTATION
___ 5. NARBOROUGH
___ 6. BASIL
___ 7. UNSELFISH
___ 8. JULIET
___ 9. CAMPBELL
___ 10. DORIAN
___ 11. ISAACS
___ 12. HENRY
___ 13. PARIS
___ 14. JAMES
___ 15. SINS
___ 16. GOOD
___ 17. LEAF
___ 18. SPHINXES
___ 19. YOUTH
___ 20. SATYR
___ 21. RINGS
___ 22. CLOUSTON
___ 23. FATHER
___ 24. OPERA
___ 25. WILDE

A. Author
B. Dorian's housekeeper
C. He has a negative influence on Dorian: Lord ___.
D. She thinks living in the country is boring.
E. Lord Henry describes women as these without secrets.
F. Basil sees this in his portrait of Dorian.
G. He murders Basil.
H. Lord Henry says these people are colorless and lack individuality.
I. He disposes of Basil's body.
J. The portrait showed this in the mouth.
K. He shoots the man hiding in the thicket.
L. Rules Sibyl's death a accident
M. Person who asks Lord Henry how to become young again
N. Dorian believes that forgiveness for these is impossible.
O. He advances Sibyl's family 50 pounds.
P. The secret of this is to repeat the follies of it.
Q. Basil wants to exhibit Dorian's portrait there.
R. According to Lord Henry, the only way to get rid of this is to yeild to it.
S. He wants to kill Dorian.
T. According to Lord Henry, to be this is to be in harmony with oneself.
U. Dorian's was killed in a duel.
V. Dorian goes there after he learns of Sibyl's death.
W. Dorian's servants can only identify his body by these.
X. Sibyl's theater role
Y. He painted the portrait of Dorian Gray.

The Picture of Dorian Gray Matching 3 Answer Key

M - 1.	DUCHESS	A. Author
J - 2.	CRUELTY	B. Dorian's housekeeper
L - 3.	CORONER	C. He has a negative influence on Dorian: Lord ___.
R - 4.	TEMPTATION	D. She thinks living in the country is boring.
D - 5.	NARBOROUGH	E. Lord Henry describes women as these without secrets.
Y - 6.	BASIL	F. Basil sees this in his portrait of Dorian.
H - 7.	UNSELFISH	G. He murders Basil.
X - 8.	JULIET	H. Lord Henry says these people are colorless and lack individuality.
I - 9.	CAMPBELL	I. He disposes of Basil's body.
G -10.	DORIAN	J. The portrait showed this in the mouth.
O -11.	ISAACS	K. He shoots the man hiding in the thicket.
C -12.	HENRY	L. Rules Sibyl's death a accident
Q -13.	PARIS	M. Person who asks Lord Henry how to become young again
S -14.	JAMES	N. Dorian believes that forgiveness for these is impossible.
N -15.	SINS	O. He advances Sibyl's family 50 pounds.
T -16.	GOOD	P. The secret of this is to repeat the follies of it.
B -17.	LEAF	Q. Basil wants to exhibit Dorian's portrait there.
E -18.	SPHINXES	R. According to Lord Henry, the only way to get rid of this is to yeild to it.
P -19.	YOUTH	S. He wants to kill Dorian.
F -20.	SATYR	T. According to Lord Henry, to be this is to be in harmony with oneself.
W -21.	RINGS	U. Dorian's was killed in a duel.
K -22.	CLOUSTON	V. Dorian goes there after he learns of Sibyl's death.
U -23.	FATHER	W. Dorian's servants can only identify his body by these.
V -24.	OPERA	X. Sibyl's theater role
A -25.	WILDE	Y. He painted the portrait of Dorian Gray.

The Picture of Dorian Gray Matching 4

___ 1. SATYR
___ 2. CAMPBELL
___ 3. LEAF
___ 4. RINGS
___ 5. ISAACS
___ 6. WAINSCOTING
___ 7. NARBOROUGH
___ 8. UNSELFISH
___ 9. BASIL
___ 10. CORONER
___ 11. DUCHESS
___ 12. YOUTH
___ 13. VANE
___ 14. SINGLETON
___ 15. WILDE
___ 16. DORIAN
___ 17. OPERA
___ 18. HETTY
___ 19. SINS
___ 20. CLOUSTON
___ 21. VICTORIA
___ 22. SOUL
___ 23. SYBIL
___ 24. BEAUTY
___ 25. TEMPTATION

A. Rules Sibyl's death a accident
B. Young peasant girl Dorian chooses to leave while she is still pure
C. Dorian claims this can be bought, sold, and bartered away.
D. She commits suicide.
E. Dorian's housekeeper
F. He disposes of Basil's body.
G. He shoots the man hiding in the thicket.
H. She thinks living in the country is boring.
I. According to Lord Henry, the only way to get rid of this is to yeild to it.
J. Lord Henry says these people are colorless and lack individuality.
K. Lord Henry tells Dorian the secret of life is the search for this.
L. Person who asks Lord Henry how to become young again
M. Dorian goes there after he learns of Sibyl's death.
N. Dorian believes that forgiveness for these is impossible.
O. He murders Basil.
P. He advances Sibyl's family 50 pounds.
Q. Author
R. Dorian hides Basil's belongings behind this.
S. Last name of Sibyl and James
T. The secret of this is to repeat the follies of it.
U. Dorian's servants can only identify his body by these.
V. He painted the portrait of Dorian Gray.
W. He sees Dorian at the opium house.
X. Basil sees this in his portrait of Dorian.
Y. Lord Henry's wife

The Picture of Dorian Gray Matching 4 Answer Key

X - 1.	SATYR	A. Rules Sibyl's death a accident
F - 2.	CAMPBELL	B. Young peasant girl Dorian chooses to leave while she is still pure
E - 3.	LEAF	C. Dorian claims this can be bought, sold, and bartered away.
U - 4.	RINGS	D. She commits suicide.
P - 5.	ISAACS	E. Dorian's housekeeper
R - 6.	WAINSCOTING	F. He disposes of Basil's body.
H - 7.	NARBOROUGH	G. He shoots the man hiding in the thicket.
J - 8.	UNSELFISH	H. She thinks living in the country is boring.
V - 9.	BASIL	I. According to Lord Henry, the only way to get rid of this is to yeild to it.
A - 10.	CORONER	J. Lord Henry says these people are colorless and lack individuality.
L - 11.	DUCHESS	K. Lord Henry tells Dorian the secret of life is the search for this.
T - 12.	YOUTH	L. Person who asks Lord Henry how to become young again
S - 13.	VANE	M. Dorian goes there after he learns of Sibyl's death.
W - 14.	SINGLETON	N. Dorian believes that forgiveness for these is impossible.
Q - 15.	WILDE	O. He murders Basil.
O - 16.	DORIAN	P. He advances Sibyl's family 50 pounds.
M - 17.	OPERA	Q. Author
B - 18.	HETTY	R. Dorian hides Basil's belongings behind this.
N - 19.	SINS	S. Last name of Sibyl and James
G - 20.	CLOUSTON	T. The secret of this is to repeat the follies of it.
Y - 21.	VICTORIA	U. Dorian's servants can only identify his body by these.
C - 22.	SOUL	V. He painted the portrait of Dorian Gray.
D - 23.	SYBIL	W. He sees Dorian at the opium house.
K - 24.	BEAUTY	X. Basil sees this in his portrait of Dorian.
I - 25.	TEMPTATION	Y. Lord Henry's wife

The Picture of Dorian Gray Magic Squares 1

Match the definition with the vocabulary word. Put your answers in the magic squares below. When your answers are correct, all columns and rows will add to the same number.

A. ERSKINE   E. REALITY   I. UGLY   M. DUCHESS
B. JULIET   F. HETTY   J. PRINCE   N. SOUL
C. YOUTH   G. PORTRAIT   K. CORONER   O. OPERA
D. CLOUSTON   H. LEAF   L. NARBOROUGH   P. VICTORIA

1. Dorian goes there after he learns of Sibyl's death.
2. Sibyl knows Dorian by this 'Charming' name
3. Dorian's housekeeper
4. He claims Lord Henry is extremely dangerous.
5. He shoots the man hiding in the thicket.
6. It spoiled Sibyl's acting.
7. Rules Sibyl's death a accident
8. Dorian claims this can be bought, sold, and bartered away.
9. Young peasant girl Dorian chooses to leave while she is still pure
10. The secret of this is to repeat the follies of it.
11. Person who asks Lord Henry how to become young again
12. She thinks living in the country is boring.
13. Lord Henry says it is better to be good than this.
14. Lord Henry's wife
15. Sibyl's theater role
16. Visual diary of Dorian's soul

A=	B=	C=	D=
E=	F=	G=	H=
I=	J=	K=	L=
M=	N=	O=	P=

21
Copyrighted

The Picture of Dorian Gray Magic Squares 1 Answer Key

Match the definition with the vocabulary word. Put your answers in the magic squares below. When your answers are correct, all columns and rows will add to the same number.

A. ERSKINE
B. JULIET
C. YOUTH
D. CLOUSTON
E. REALITY
F. HETTY
G. PORTRAIT
H. LEAF
I. UGLY
J. PRINCE
K. CORONER
L. NARBOROUGH
M. DUCHESS
N. SOUL
O. OPERA
P. VICTORIA

1. Dorian goes there after he learns of Sibyl's death.
2. Sibyl knows Dorian by this 'Charming' name
3. Dorian's housekeeper
4. He claims Lord Henry is extremely dangerous.
5. He shoots the man hiding in the thicket.
6. It spoiled Sibyl's acting.
7. Rules Sibyl's death a accident
8. Dorian claims this can be bought, sold, and bartered away.
9. Young peasant girl Dorian chooses to leave while she is still pure
10. The secret of this is to repeat the follies of it.
11. Person who asks Lord Henry how to become young again
12. She thinks living in the country is boring.
13. Lord Henry says it is better to be good than this.
14. Lord Henry's wife
15. Sibyl's theater role
16. Visual diary of Dorian's soul

A=4	B=15	C=10	D=5
E=6	F=9	G=16	H=3
I=13	J=2	K=7	L=12
M=11	N=8	O=1	P=14

The Picture of Dorian Gray Magic Squares 2

Match the definition with the vocabulary word. Put your answers in the magic squares below. When your answers are correct, all columns and rows will add to the same number.

A. VANE
B. OPERA
C. PRINCE
D. UNSELFISH
E. CORONER
F. WAINSCOTING
G. TEMPTATION
H. SATYR
I. DUCHESS
J. PORTRAIT
K. BASIL
L. YOUTH
M. HENRY
N. BERWICK
O. WILDE
P. ERSKINE

1. Sibyl knows Dorian by this 'Charming' name
2. Visual diary of Dorian's soul
3. Dorian hides Basil's belongings behind this.
4. Author
5. He claims Lord Henry is extremely dangerous.
6. Rules Sibyl's death a accident
7. Person who asks Lord Henry how to become young again
8. Lord Henry says these people are colorless and lack individuality.
9. He has a negative influence on Dorian: Lord ___.
10. Basil sees this in his portrait of Dorian.
11. The secret of this is to repeat the follies of it.
12. Last name of Sibyl and James.
13. Dorian goes there after he learns of Sibyl's death.
14. He painted the portrait of Dorian Gray.
15. According to Lord Henry, the only way to get rid of this is to yeild to it.
16. He leaves the smoking room when Dorian arrives.

A=	B=	C=	D=
E=	F=	G=	H=
I=	J=	K=	L=
M=	N=	O=	P=

The Picture of Dorian Gray Magic Squares 2 Answer Key

Match the definition with the vocabulary word. Put your answers in the magic squares below. When your answers are correct, all columns and rows will add to the same number.

A. VANE
B. OPERA
C. PRINCE
D. UNSELFISH
E. CORONER
F. WAINSCOTING
G. TEMPTATION
H. SATYR
I. DUCHESS
J. PORTRAIT
K. BASIL
L. YOUTH
M. HENRY
N. BERWICK
O. WILDE
P. ERSKINE

1. Sibyl knows Dorian by this 'Charming' name
2. Visual diary of Dorian's soul
3. Dorian hides Basil's belongings behind this.
4. Author
5. He claims Lord Henry is extremely dangerous.
6. Rules Sibyl's death a accident
7. Person who asks Lord Henry how to become young again
8. Lord Henry says these people are colorless and lack individuality.
9. He has a negative influence on Dorian: Lord ___.
10. Basil sees this in his portrait of Dorian.
11. The secret of this is to repeat the follies of it.
12. Last name of Sibyl and James
13. Dorian goes there after he learns of Sibyl's death.
14. He painted the portrait of Dorian Gray.
15. According to Lord Henry, the only way to get rid of this is to yeild to it.
16. He leaves the smoking room when Dorian arrives.

A=12	B=13	C=1	D=8
E=6	F=3	G=15	H=10
I=7	J=2	K=14	L=11
M=9	N=16	O=4	P=5

The Picture of Dorian Gray Magic Squares 3

Match the definition with the vocabulary word. Put your answers in the magic squares below. When your answers are correct, all columns and rows will add to the same number.

A. SYBIL
B. CLOUSTON
C. VANE
D. YOUTH
E. ERSKINE
F. UNSELFISH
G. SINGLETON
H. ISAACS
I. SOUL
J. NARBOROUGH
K. SATYR
L. LEAF
M. UGLY
N. JULIET
O. OPERA
P. DORIAN

1. She commits suicide.
2. Sibyl's theater role
3. She thinks living in the country is boring.
4. He claims Lord Henry is extremely dangerous.
5. He sees Dorian at the opium house.
6. Dorian's housekeeper
7. He murders Basil.
8. Last name of Sibyl and James
9. Dorian goes there after he learns of Sibyl's death.
10. The secret of this is to repeat the follies of it.
11. He advances Sibyl's family 50 pounds.
12. Basil sees this in his portrait of Dorian.
13. Dorian claims this can be bought, sold, and bartered away.
14. Lord Henry says these people are colorless and lack individuality.
15. He shoots the man hiding in the thicket.
16. Lord Henry says it is better to be good than this.

A=	B=	C=	D=
E=	F=	G=	H=
I=	J=	K=	L=
M=	N=	O=	P=

The Picture of Dorian Gray Magic Squares 3 Answer Key

Match the definition with the vocabulary word. Put your answers in the magic squares below. When your answers are correct, all columns and rows will add to the same number.

A. SYBIL
B. CLOUSTON
C. VANE
D. YOUTH
E. ERSKINE
F. UNSELFISH
G. SINGLETON
H. ISAACS
I. SOUL
J. NARBOROUGH
K. SATYR
L. LEAF
M. UGLY
N. JULIET
O. OPERA
P. DORIAN

1. She commits suicide.
2. Sibyl's theater role
3. She thinks living in the country is boring.
4. He claims Lord Henry is extremely dangerous.
5. He sees Dorian at the opium house.
6. Dorian's housekeeper
7. He murders Basil.
8. Last name of Sibyl and James
9. Dorian goes there after he learns of Sibyl's death.
10. The secret of this is to repeat the follies of it.
11. He advances Sibyl's family 50 pounds.
12. Basil sees this in his portrait of Dorian.
13. Dorian claims this can be bought, sold, and bartered away.
14. Lord Henry says these people are colorless and lack individuality.
15. He shoots the man hiding in the thicket.
16. Lord Henry says it is better to be good than this.

A=1	B=15	C=8	D=10
E=4	F=14	G=5	H=11
I=13	J=3	K=12	L=6
M=16	N=2	O=9	P=7

The Picture of Dorian Gray Magic Squares 4

Match the definition with the vocabulary word. Put your answers in the magic squares below. When your answers are correct, all columns and rows will add to the same number.

A. SINS
B. BOOK
C. SINGLETON
D. CORONER
E. VANE
F. DORIAN
G. PARIS
H. CRUELTY
I. UNSELFISH
J. DUCHESS
K. ISAACS
L. NARBOROUGH
M. HETTY
N. RINGS
O. YOUTH
P. BERWICK

1. He murders Basil.
2. Lord Henry says these people are colorless and lack individuality.
3. The secret of this is to repeat the follies of it.
4. Rules Sibyl's death a accident
5. Young peasant girl Dorian chooses to leave while she is still pure
6. It has a huge influence on Dorian's behavior.
7. The portrait showed this in the mouth.
8. He advances Sibyl's family 50 pounds.
9. He sees Dorian at the opium house.
10. He leaves the smoking room when Dorian arrives.
11. Person who asks Lord Henry how to become young again
12. Last name of Sibyl and James
13. She thinks living in the country is boring.
14. Basil wants to exhibit Dorian's portrait there.
15. Dorian believes that forgiveness for these is impossible.
16. Dorian's servants can only identify his body by these.

A=	B=	C=	D=
E=	F=	G=	H=
I=	J=	K=	L=
M=	N=	O=	P=

The Picture of Dorian Gray Magic Squares 4 Answer Key

Match the definition with the vocabulary word. Put your answers in the magic squares below. When your answers are correct, all columns and rows will add to the same number.

A. SINS
B. BOOK
C. SINGLETON
D. CORONER
E. VANE
F. DORIAN
G. PARIS
H. CRUELTY
I. UNSELFISH
J. DUCHESS
K. ISAACS
L. NARBOROUGH
M. HETTY
N. RINGS
O. YOUTH
P. BERWICK

1. He murders Basil.
2. Lord Henry says these people are colorless and lack individuality.
3. The secret of this is to repeat the follies of it.
4. Rules Sibyl's death a accident
5. Young peasant girl Dorian chooses to leave while she is still pure
6. It has a huge influence on Dorian's behavior.
7. The portrait showed this in the mouth.
8. He advances Sibyl's family 50 pounds.
9. He sees Dorian at the opium house.
10. He leaves the smoking room when Dorian arrives.
11. Person who asks Lord Henry how to become young again
12. Last name of Sibyl and James
13. She thinks living in the country is boring.
14. Basil wants to exhibit Dorian's portrait there.
15. Dorian believes that forgiveness for these is impossible.
16. Dorian's servants can only identify his body by these.

A=15	B=6	C=9	D=4
E=12	F=1	G=14	H=7
I=2	J=11	K=8	L=13
M=5	N=16	O=3	P=10

The Picture of Dorian Gray Word Search 1

```
U N S E L F I S H S O U L Y O U T H
H R M N E Y C Y N I Y W Z P F E W X
B C N A A Y F I B N F B M D I W I Y
B A V V F Z S S V G S H I L D A L G
M B S I R A P U G L Y N U L U I D D
R E N I S O Z C M E O J Q V C N E S
Y R P T L G P F G T D Z Y Z H S R W
R W W E B Z C E S O F O S X E C E S
E I D M S S P U R N P D R T S O N R
A C G P D H O J S A H H I I S T O Y
L K F T M L A A H P A A N X A I R N
I S A A C S T M F Y R I N G S N O Y
T K L T T Y H E E T E I O G E G C Y
Y N S I R H F S R T J O N H W N Q F
Q G D O Q M E O G E D S C C B O O K
W K M N L V P R K H Y T U A E B C M
```

According to Lord Henry, the only way to get rid of this is to yeild to it. (10)
According to Lord Henry, to be this is to be in harmony with oneself. (4)
Author (5)
Basil sees this in his portrait of Dorian. (5)
Basil wants to exhibit Dorian's portrait there. (5)
Dorian begs Sir Geoffrey not to shoot this. (4)
Dorian believes that forgiveness for these is impossible. (4)
Dorian chooses to allow the painting to bear the burden of his ___. (5)
Dorian claims this can be bought, sold, and bartered away. (4)
Dorian goes there after he learns of Sibyl's death. (5)
Dorian hides Basil's belongings behind this. (11)
Dorian's housekeeper (4)
Dorian's servants can only identify his body by these. (5)
Dorian's was killed in a duel. (6)
He advances Sibyl's family 50 pounds. (6)
He has a negative influence on Dorian: Lord ___. (5)
He leaves the smoking room when Dorian arrives. (7)
He murders Basil. (6)
He painted the portrait of Dorian Gray. (5)
He sees Dorian at the opium house. (9)
He shoots the man hiding in the thicket. (8)
He wants to kill Dorian. (5)
It has a huge influence on Dorian's behavior. (4)
It spoiled Sibyl's acting. (7)
Last name of Sibyl and James (4)
Lord Henry says it is better to be good than this. (4)
Lord Henry says these people are colorless and lack individuality. (9)
Lord Henry tells Dorian the secret of life is the search for this. (6)
Person who asks Lord Henry how to become young again (7)
Rules Sibyl's death a accident (7)
She commits suicide. (5)
Sibyl knows Dorian by this 'Charming' name (6)
Sibyl's theater role (6)
The secret of this is to repeat the follies of it. (5)
Visual diary of Dorian's soul (8)
Young peasant girl Dorian chooses to leave while she is still pure (5)

The Picture of Dorian Gray Word Search 1 Answer Key

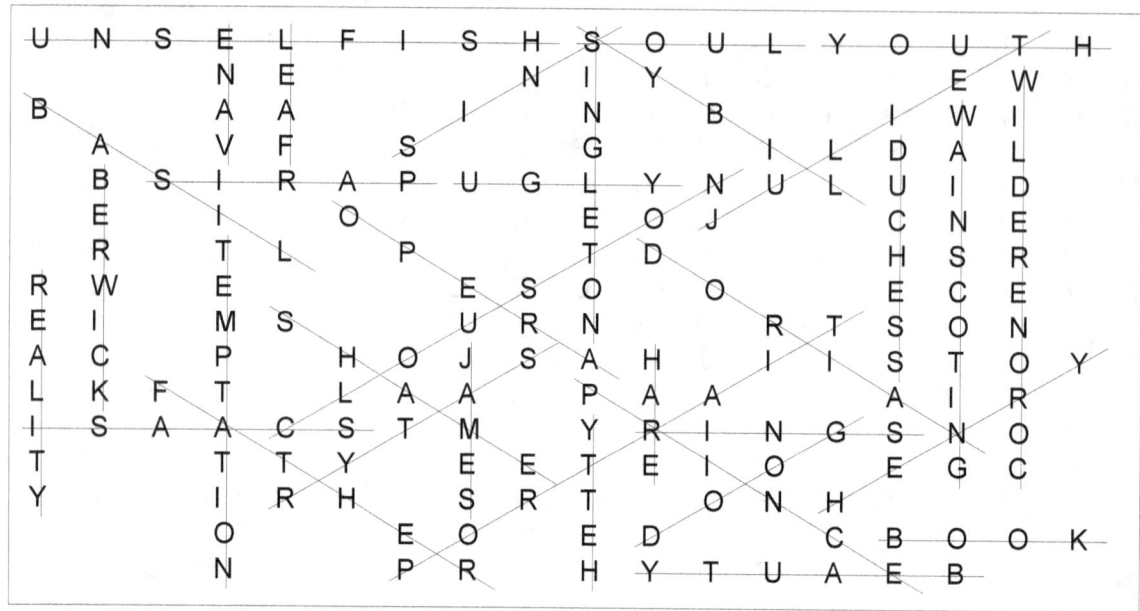

According to Lord Henry, the only way to get rid of this is to yeild to it. (10)
According to Lord Henry, to be this is to be in harmony with oneself. (4)
Author (5)
Basil sees this in his portrait of Dorian. (5)
Basil wants to exhibit Dorian's portrait there. (5)
Dorian begs Sir Geoffrey not to shoot this. (4)
Dorian believes that forgiveness for these is impossible. (4)
Dorian chooses to allow the painting to bear the burden of his ___. (5)
Dorian claims this can be bought, sold, and bartered away. (4)
Dorian goes there after he learns of Sibyl's death. (5)
Dorian hides Basil's belongings behind this. (11)
Dorian's housekeeper (4)
Dorian's servants can only identify his body by these. (5)
Dorian's was killed in a duel. (6)
He advances Sibyl's family 50 pounds. (6)
He has a negative influence on Dorian: Lord ___. (5)
He leaves the smoking room when Dorian arrives. (7)

He murders Basil. (6)
He painted the portrait of Dorian Gray. (5)
He sees Dorian at the opium house. (9)
He shoots the man hiding in the thicket. (8)
He wants to kill Dorian. (5)
It has a huge influence on Dorian's behavior. (4)
It spoiled Sibyl's acting. (7)
Last name of Sibyl and James (4)
Lord Henry says it is better to be good than this. (4)
Lord Henry says these people are colorless and lack individuality. (9)
Lord Henry tells Dorian the secret of life is the search for this. (6)
Person who asks Lord Henry how to become young again (7)
Rules Sibyl's death a accident (7)
She commits suicide. (5)
Sibyl knows Dorian by this 'Charming' name (6)
Sibyl's theater role (6)
The secret of this is to repeat the follies of it. (5)
Visual diary of Dorian's soul (8)
Young peasant girl Dorian chooses to leave while she is still pure (5)

The Picture of Dorian Gray Word Search 2

```
S G N I R W A I N S C O T I N G L V
N Y N Q E B J H P R A P N R V I H E
Z T D M A V T U U N M E A H S V M T
B T T J L W S E L O P R R A E A L F
W E Z G I X L P M I B A B G H N K Y
Y H A L T T P A S T E X O S O E R V
Z T D U Y G R R O A L T R C Q O Z Y
L E R Z T G C I U T L N O A H F D F
P E N X E Y C S L P R Q U A K A P C
Q B A L X H X K K M H B G S Q T R P
W B E F T U G L Y E S A H I L H I X
F T M U S Y B I L T V B R S T E N Z
C L O U S T O N C O R O N E R R C W
C Y P W Z P O R T R A I T M T T E P
S E R S K I N E W H S T S A T Y R F
J F L C D O R I A N Y D T J B O O K
```

According to Lord Henry, the only way to get rid of this is to yeild to it. (10)
According to Lord Henry, to be this is to be in harmony with oneself. (4)
Author (5)
Basil sees this in his portrait of Dorian. (5)
Basil wants to exhibit Dorian's portrait there. (5)
Dorian begs Sir Geoffrey not to shoot this. (4)
Dorian believes that forgiveness for these is impossible. (4)
Dorian chooses to allow the painting to bear the burden of his ___. (5)
Dorian claims this can be bought, sold, and bartered away. (4)
Dorian goes there after he learns of Sibyl's death. (5)
Dorian hides Basil's belongings behind this. (11)
Dorian sends one to Lord Henry announcing his engagement. (8)
Dorian's housekeeper (4)
Dorian's servants can only identify his body by these. (5)
Dorian's was killed in a duel. (6)
He advances Sibyl's family 50 pounds. (6)
He claims Lord Henry is extremely dangerous. (7)

He disposes of Basil's body. (8)
He has a negative influence on Dorian: Lord ___. (5)
He murders Basil. (6)
He painted the portrait of Dorian Gray. (5)
He shoots the man hiding in the thicket. (8)
He wants to kill Dorian. (5)
It has a huge influence on Dorian's behavior. (4)
It spoiled Sibyl's acting. (7)
Last name of Sibyl and James (4)
Lord Henry says it is better to be good than this. (4)
Lord Henry tells Dorian the secret of life is the search for this. (6)
Rules Sibyl's death a accident (7)
She commits suicide. (5)
She thinks living in the country is boring. (10)
Sibyl knows Dorian by this 'Charming' name (6)
Sibyl's theater role (6)
The portrait showed this in the mouth. (7)
The secret of this is to repeat the follies of it. (5)
Visual diary of Dorian's soul (8)
Young peasant girl Dorian chooses to leave while she is still pure (5)

The Picture of Dorian Gray Word Search 2 Answer Key

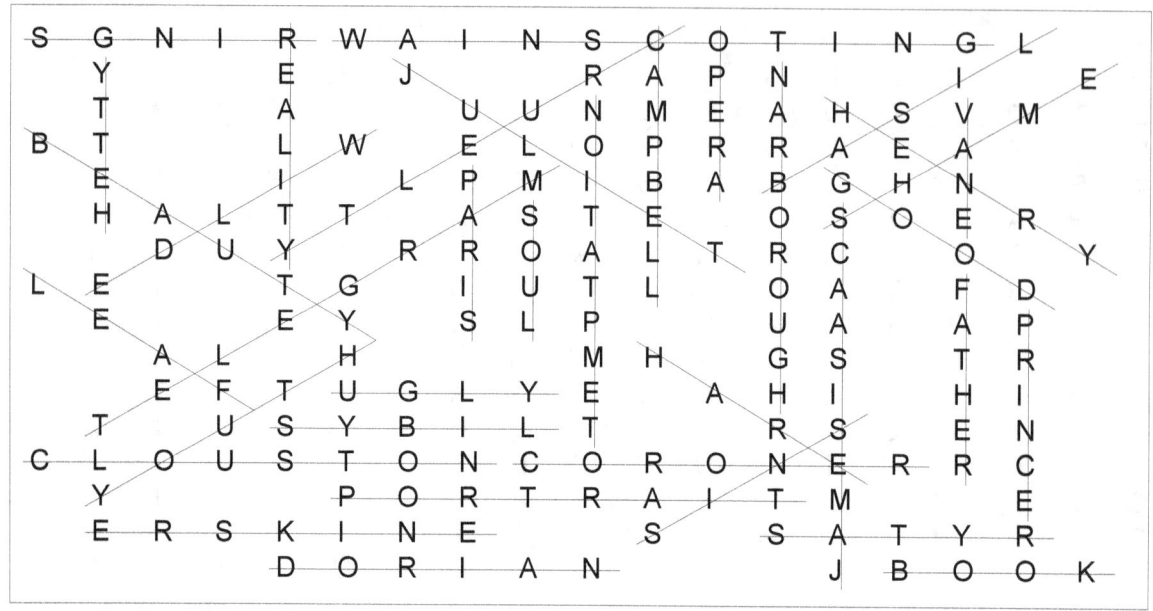

According to Lord Henry, the only way to get rid of this is to yeild to it. (10)
According to Lord Henry, to be this is to be in harmony with oneself. (4)
Author (5)
Basil sees this in his portrait of Dorian. (5)
Basil wants to exhibit Dorian's portrait there. (5)
Dorian begs Sir Geoffrey not to shoot this. (4)
Dorian believes that forgiveness for these is impossible. (4)
Dorian chooses to allow the painting to bear the burden of his ___. (5)
Dorian claims this can be bought, sold, and bartered away. (4)
Dorian goes there after he learns of Sibyl's death. (5)
Dorian hides Basil's belongings behind this. (11)
Dorian sends one to Lord Henry announcing his engagement. (8)
Dorian's housekeeper (4)
Dorian's servants can only identify his body by these. (5)
Dorian's was killed in a duel. (6)
He advances Sibyl's family 50 pounds. (6)
He claims Lord Henry is extremely dangerous. (7)

He disposes of Basil's body. (8)
He has a negative influence on Dorian: Lord ___. (5)
He murders Basil. (6)
He painted the portrait of Dorian Gray. (5)
He shoots the man hiding in the thicket. (8)
He wants to kill Dorian. (5)
It has a huge influence on Dorian's behavior. (4)
It spoiled Sibyl's acting. (7)
Last name of Sibyl and James (4)
Lord Henry says it is better to be good than this. (4)
Lord Henry tells Dorian the secret of life is the search for this. (6)
Rules Sibyl's death a accident (7)
She commits suicide. (5)
She thinks living in the country is boring. (10)
Sibyl knows Dorian by this 'Charming' name (6)
Sibyl's theater role (6)
The portrait showed this in the mouth. (7)
The secret of this is to repeat the follies of it. (5)
Visual diary of Dorian's soul (8)
Young peasant girl Dorian chooses to leave while she is still pure (5)

The Picture of Dorian Gray Word Search 3

```
N J U L I E T C J E F D G P S O P E R A
O A P R F N S B L J R A O S M Y Z R H X
I W R A Z T Y E R O C S T R H K B V Y Q
T A B B R M J A S U L K H I C S I L Q
A I U A O I K U G J X S P I E A B C L N
T N N P S R S T G X K B T Y N R N T E J
P S S M T I O Y S O N H N O B E M O B B
M C E P T B L U M Y O P R I N C E R P G
E O L O H S B N G N G D F K N Z D I M N
T T F R M I N M Y H F J Q S T G U A A P
Y I I T Q H N S I N S Z C K F R C L C L
N N S R Q E P X H X Z A F X X L H Z T L
K G H A P T R N E W A L Y B B N E N Z V
T K L I B T L F C S L G X H H F S S W F
M P R T N Y H N I R B W M K V G S T S L
P F H W L P S M P R H P W Y P Y F I D
X P C F D S V X X G P N Z W Y K K P N Z
Z G L G H R F Q N C P R M Q G C G J G Z
D C J K H X K W O M C N X S Y R M P L S
G L H R X C Y R Q C F H G T L P R E R
S N E Z I S O Z T J A W E N I H Y J T G
K T N W M N U V C T E D X I L T A M O E
O C R U E L T Y T E L G R A M T R N H
O E Y R J T H Z D I W C V S E N Y A E T
B U G L Y H T J W E M A H S R X V Z N F
```

BASIL	FATHER	PARIS	SYBIL
BEAUTY	GOOD	PORTRAIT	TELEGRAM
BERWICK	HARE	PRINCE	TEMPTATION
BOOK	HENRY	REALITY	UGLY
CAMPBELL	HETTY	RINGS	UNSELFISH
CLOUSTON	ISAACS	SATYR	VANE
CORONER	JAMES	SHAME	VICTORIA
CRUELTY	JULIET	SINGLETON	WAINSCOTING
DORIAN	LEAF	SINS	WILDE
DUCHESS	NARBOROUGH	SOUL	YOUTH
ERSKINE	OPERA	SPHINXES	

The Picture of Dorian Gray Word Search 3 Answer Key

BASIL	FATHER	PARIS	SYBIL
BEAUTY	GOOD	PORTRAIT	TELEGRAM
BERWICK	HARE	PRINCE	TEMPTATION
BOOK	HENRY	REALITY	UGLY
CAMPBELL	HETTY	RINGS	UNSELFISH
CLOUSTON	ISAACS	SATYR	VANE
CORONER	JAMES	SHAME	VICTORIA
CRUELTY	JULIET	SINGLETON	WAINSCOTING
DORIAN	LEAF	SINS	WILDE
DUCHESS	NARBOROUGH	SOUL	YOUTH
ERSKINE	OPERA	SPHINXES	

The Picture of Dorian Gray Word Search 4

```
S C A A S I W A I N S C O T I N G N S Q
H I P J I D Z D L N S X P L T Y G A H T
A U N Q N J G T O T G H E X I G T R W D
R N B G S J P R C R N Z R Q A Y O B I Q
E S K O L E A F Y T I L A E R E D O L P
B E O V O E G M A S R A M E T R U R D F
A L T U P K T H Z T Z P N B R S C O E X
S F Q E L G D O R K H O V E O K H U Q F
I I W E M A H S N A R E X R P I E G D G
L S T W W P Y N I O S T R W T N S H Y K
H H N B C B T R C K Q R M I F E S D Y Z
T P Y C I B O A B R H M F C H V F N J P
X N J L X T W V T P V H F K T Y V S Y L
C N B D C F G A B I T W V H T T R V C W
Y T S I W B N N N U O V Z L Y R Q V B X
Z S V J F V T E O Y Z N E Z X K W L Z T
N Q P H Z P H Y G G Q U K R X J P N S Z
B M V Q W V N L L W R K P Q J L F P S K
S S P D Q C X B L C K Z H J Y K H T D X
D M K Y N K T T E J R K Y E V I P J H K
H G G W Y E K X B P A B T T N Z F X N B
D J S F I M H K P A L M T X B R S X N Y
P T E L E G R A M R B B E A U T Y C L H
L Y U Z V H M S A I N S H S D B B G K P
W J P R I N C E C S K F N O T S U O L C
```

BASIL	FATHER	PARIS	SYBIL
BEAUTY	GOOD	PORTRAIT	TELEGRAM
BERWICK	HARE	PRINCE	TEMPTATION
BOOK	HENRY	REALITY	UGLY
CAMPBELL	HETTY	RINGS	UNSELFISH
CLOUSTON	ISAACS	SATYR	VANE
CORONER	JAMES	SHAME	VICTORIA
CRUELTY	JULIET	SINGLETON	WAINSCOTING
DORIAN	LEAF	SINS	WILDE
DUCHESS	NARBOROUGH	SOUL	YOUTH
ERSKINE	OPERA	SPHINXES	

The Picture of Dorian Gray Word Search 4 Answer Key

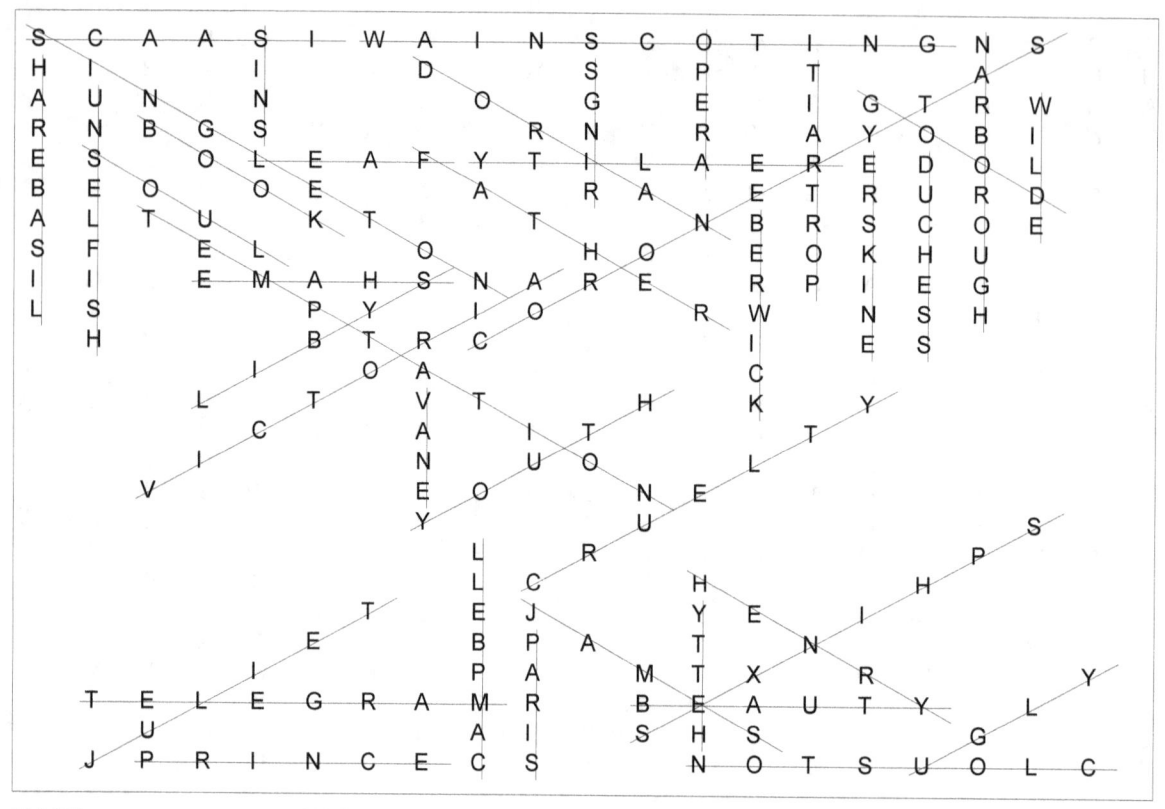

BASIL	FATHER	PARIS	SYBIL
BEAUTY	GOOD	PORTRAIT	TELEGRAM
BERWICK	HARE	PRINCE	TEMPTATION
BOOK	HENRY	REALITY	UGLY
CAMPBELL	HETTY	RINGS	UNSELFISH
CLOUSTON	ISAACS	SATYR	VANE
CORONER	JAMES	SHAME	VICTORIA
CRUELTY	JULIET	SINGLETON	WAINSCOTING
DORIAN	LEAF	SINS	WILDE
DUCHESS	NARBOROUGH	SOUL	YOUTH
ERSKINE	OPERA	SPHINXES	

The Picture of Dorian Gray Crossword 1

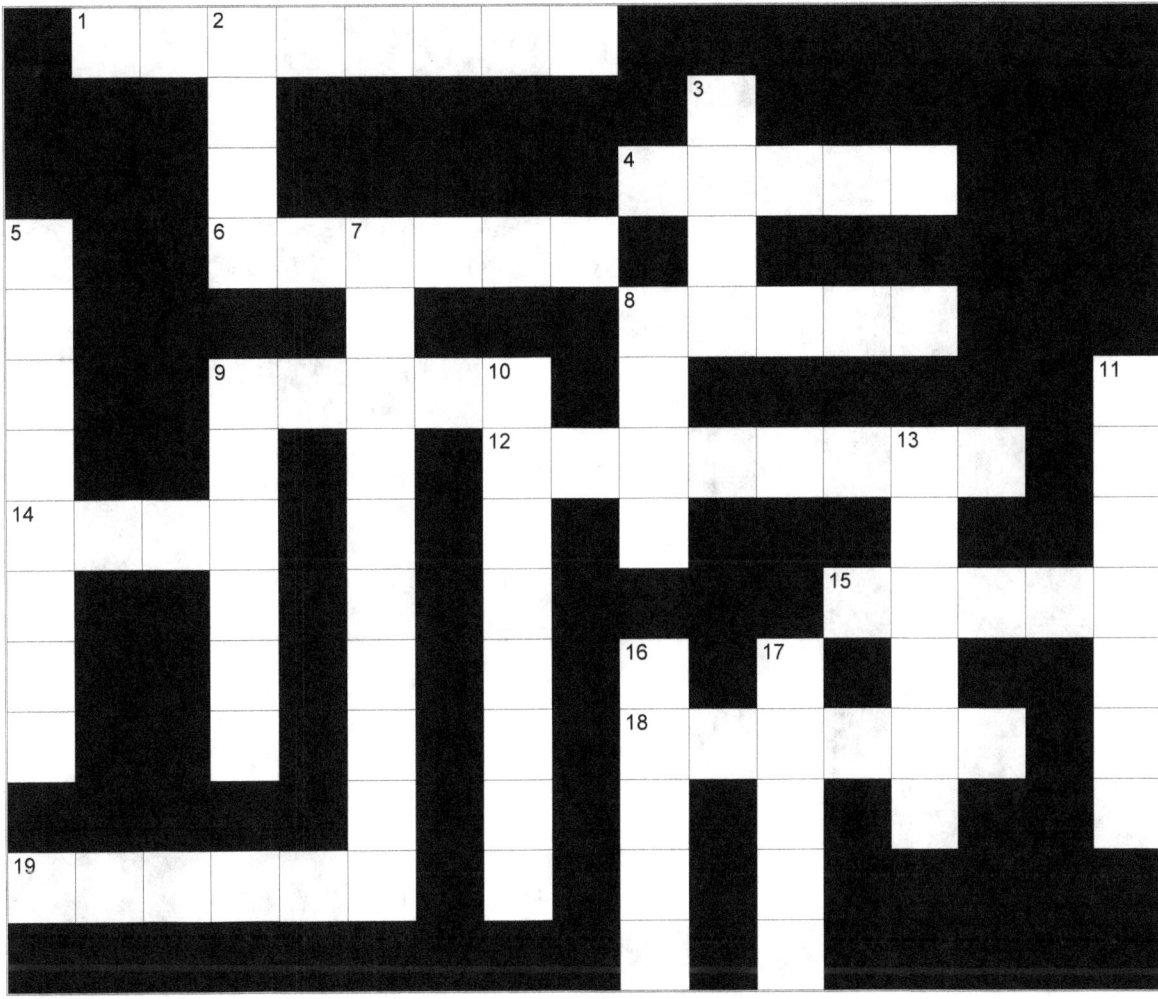

Across
1. Dorian sends one to Lord Henry announcing his engagement.
4. Basil sees this in his portrait of Dorian.
6. Dorian's was killed in a duel.
8. He has a negative influence on Dorian: Lord ___.
9. He wants to kill Dorian.
12. Visual diary of Dorian's soul
14. Dorian claims this can be bought, sold, and bartered away.
15. He painted the portrait of Dorian Gray.
18. Sibyl knows Dorian by this 'Charming' name
19. He murders Basil.

Down
2. Dorian's housekeeper
3. Last name of Sibyl and James
5. He shoots the man hiding in the thicket.
7. According to Lord Henry, the only way to get rid of this is to yeild to it.
8. Dorian begs Sir Geoffrey not to shoot this.
9. Sibyl's theater role
10. Lord Henry describes women as these without secrets.
11. It spoiled Sibyl's acting.
13. He advances Sibyl's family 50 pounds.
16. Dorian goes there after he learns of Sibyl's death.
17. Author

The Picture of Dorian Gray Crossword 1 Answer Key

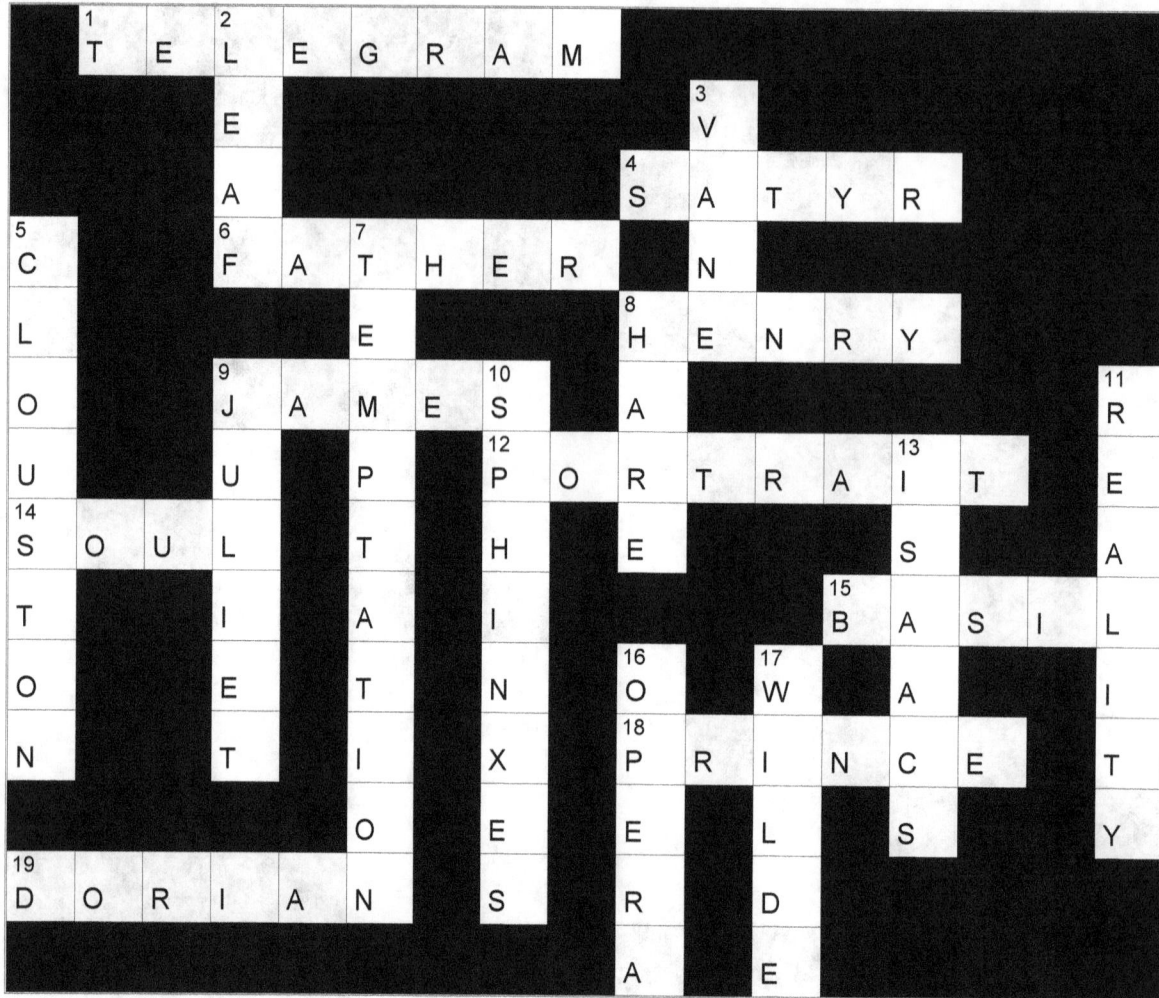

Across
1. Dorian sends one to Lord Henry announcing his engagement.
4. Basil sees this in his portrait of Dorian.
6. Dorian's was killed in a duel.
8. He has a negative influence on Dorian: Lord ___.
9. He wants to kill Dorian.
12. Visual diary of Dorian's soul
14. Dorian claims this can be bought, sold, and bartered away.
15. He painted the portrait of Dorian Gray.
18. Sibyl knows Dorian by this 'Charming' name
19. He murders Basil.

Down
2. Dorian's housekeeper
3. Last name of Sibyl and James
5. He shoots the man hiding in the thicket.
7. According to Lord Henry, the only way to get rid of this is to yeild to it.
8. Dorian begs Sir Geoffrey not to shoot this.
9. Sibyl's theater role
10. Lord Henry describes women as these without secrets.
11. It spoiled Sibyl's acting.
13. He advances Sibyl's family 50 pounds.
16. Dorian goes there after he learns of Sibyl's death.
17. Author

The Picture of Dorian Gray Crossword 2

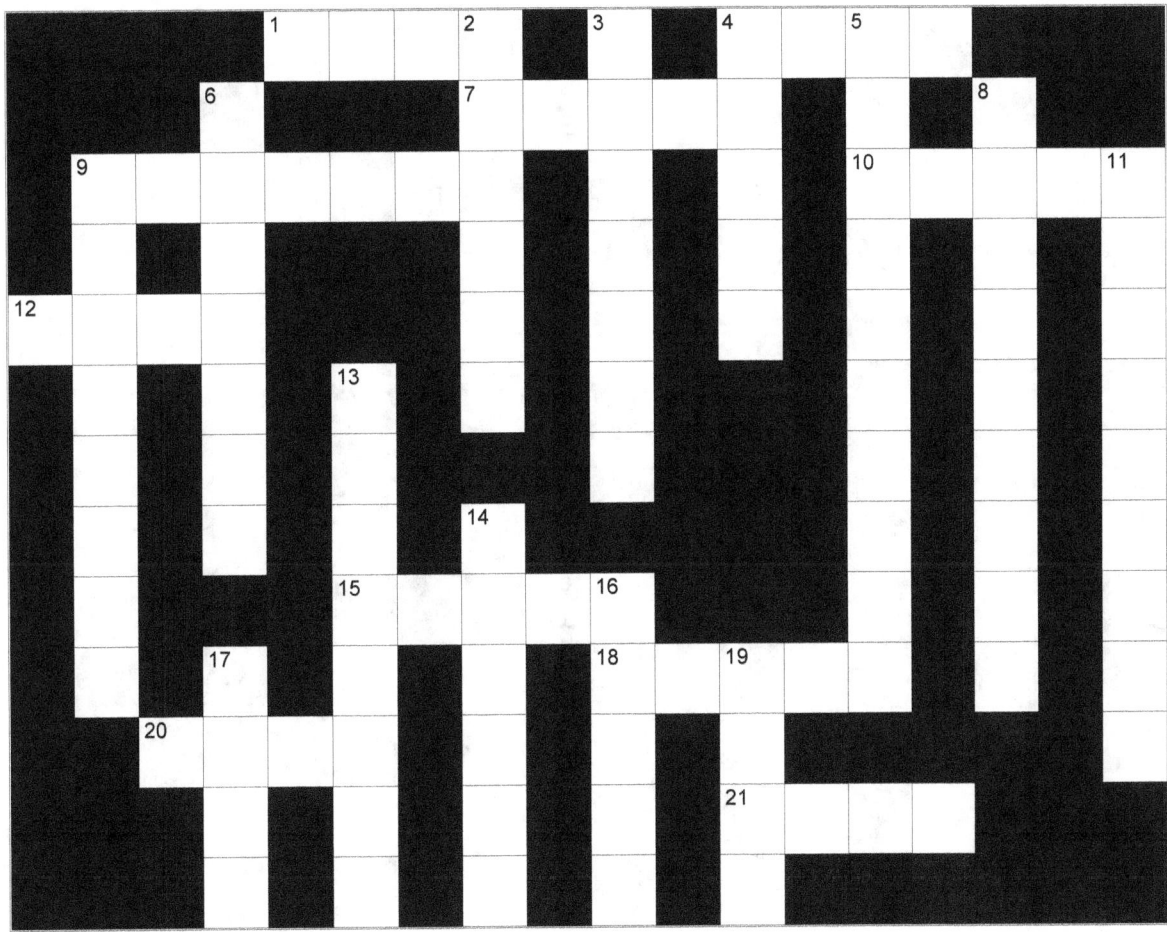

Across
1. According to Lord Henry, to be this is to be in harmony with oneself.
4. Dorian believes that forgiveness for these is impossible.
7. Dorian goes there after he learns of Sibyl's death.
9. Rules Sibyl's death a accident
10. Dorian's servants can only identify his body by these.
12. It has a huge influence on Dorian's behavior.
15. Basil wants to exhibit Dorian's portrait there.
18. The secret of this is to repeat the follies of it.
20. Dorian begs Sir Geoffrey not to shoot this.
21. Dorian's housekeeper

Down
2. He murders Basil.
3. It spoiled Sibyl's acting.
4. Basil sees this in his portrait of Dorian.
5. She thinks living in the country is boring.
6. He claims Lord Henry is extremely dangerous.
8. Lord Henry says these people are colorless and lack individuality.
9. He shoots the man hiding in the thicket.
11. He sees Dorian at the opium house.
13. He disposes of Basil's body.
14. Sibyl knows Dorian by this 'Charming' name
16. She commits suicide.
17. Last name of Sibyl and James
19. Lord Henry says it is better to be good than this.

The Picture of Dorian Gray Crossword 2 Answer Key

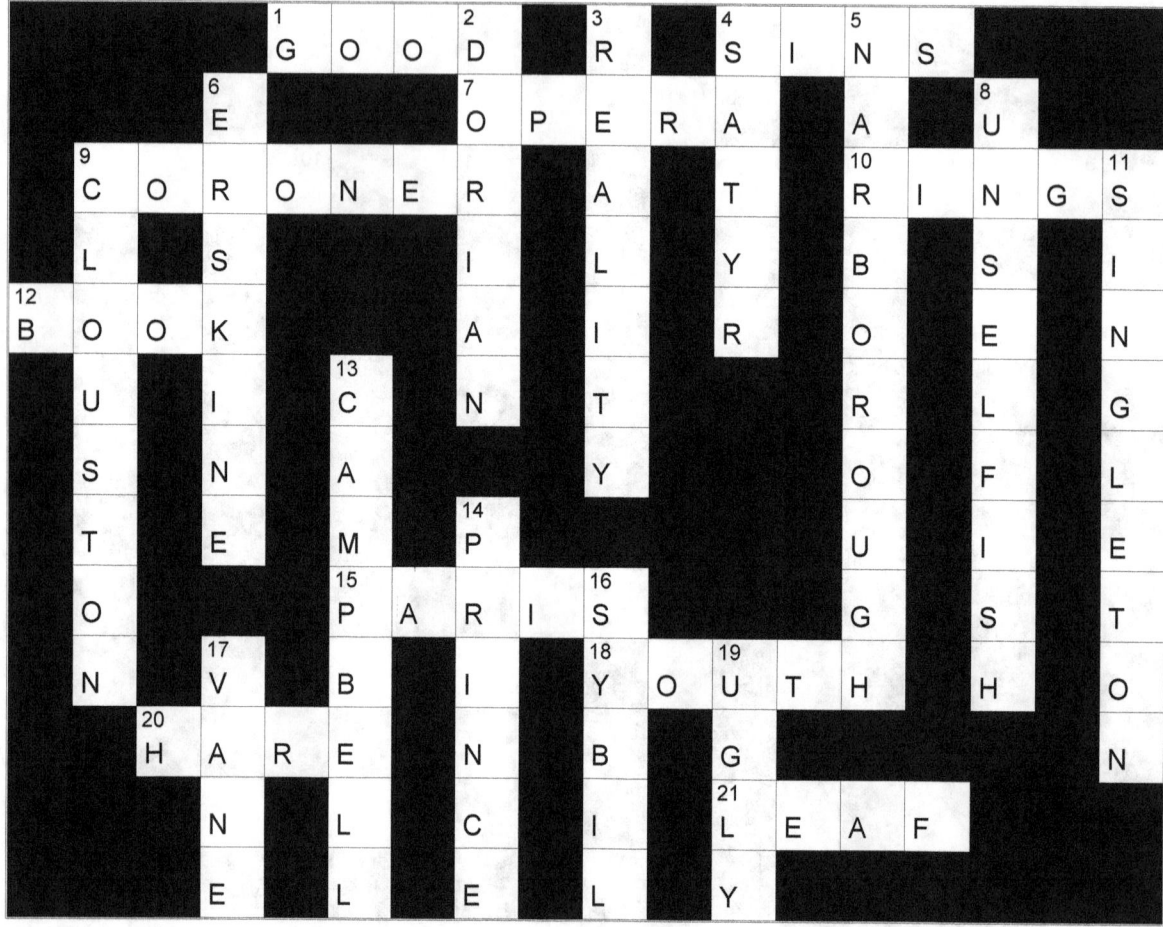

Across
1. According to Lord Henry, to be this is to be in harmony with oneself.
4. Dorian believes that forgiveness for these is impossible.
7. Dorian goes there after he learns of Sibyl's death.
9. Rules Sibyl's death a accident
10. Dorian's servants can only identify his body by these.
12. It has a huge influence on Dorian's behavior.
15. Basil wants to exhibit Dorian's portrait there.
18. The secret of this is to repeat the follies of it.
20. Dorian begs Sir Geoffrey not to shoot this.
21. Dorian's housekeeper

Down
2. He murders Basil.
3. It spoiled Sibyl's acting.
4. Basil sees this in his portrait of Dorian.
5. She thinks living in the country is boring.
6. He claims Lord Henry is extremely dangerous.
8. Lord Henry says these people are colorless and lack individuality.
9. He shoots the man hiding in the thicket.
11. He sees Dorian at the opium house.
13. He disposes of Basil's body.
14. Sibyl knows Dorian by this 'Charming' name
16. She commits suicide.
17. Last name of Sibyl and James
19. Lord Henry says it is better to be good than this.

The Picture of Dorian Gray Crossword 3

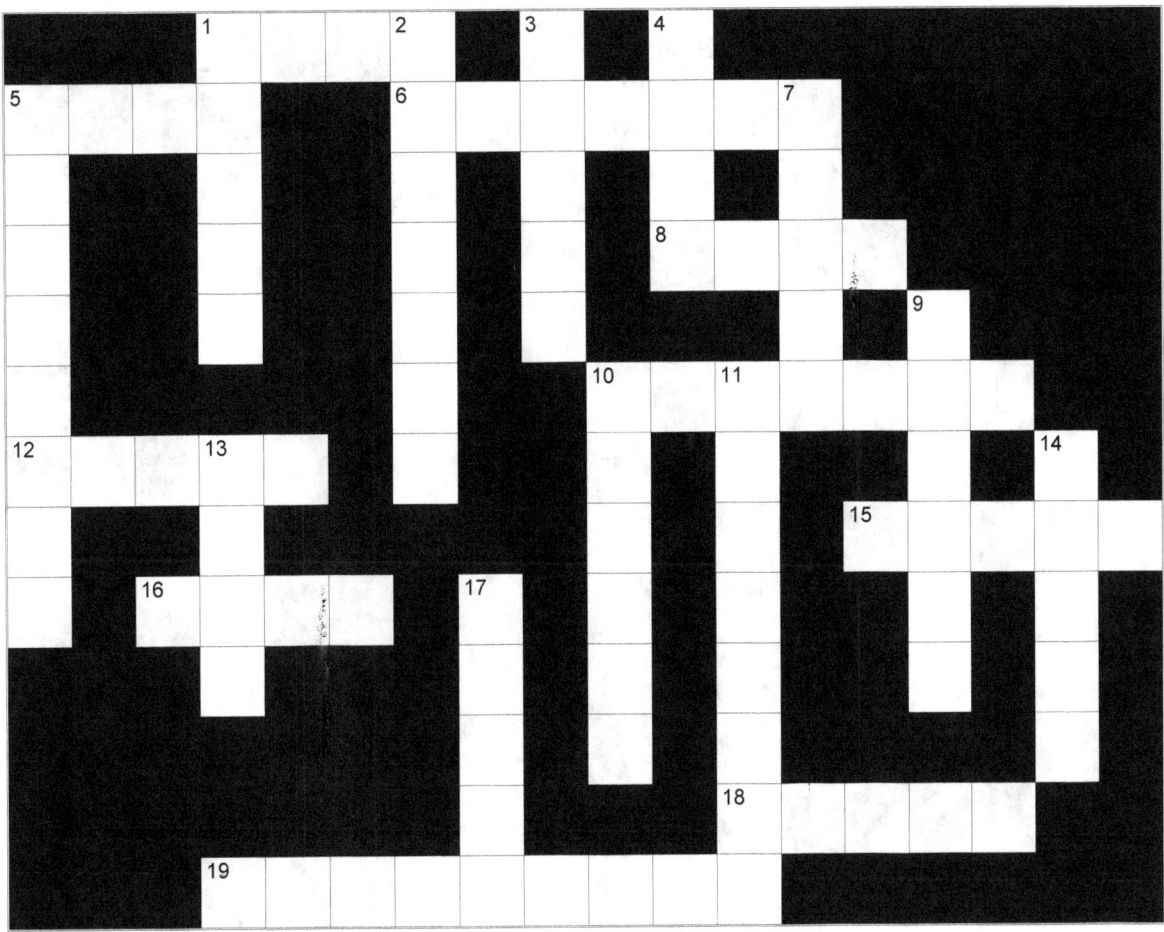

Across
1. Dorian begs Sir Geoffrey not to shoot this.
5. Last name of Sibyl and James
6. It spoiled Sibyl's acting.
8. Dorian claims this can be bought, sold, and bartered away.
10. Person who asks Lord Henry how to become young again
12. Dorian's servants can only identify his body by these.
15. Basil wants to exhibit Dorian's portrait there.
16. It has a huge influence on Dorian's behavior.
18. Dorian goes there after he learns of Sibyl's death.
19. He sees Dorian at the opium house.

Down
1. He has a negative influence on Dorian: Lord ___.
2. He claims Lord Henry is extremely dangerous.
3. Basil sees this in his portrait of Dorian.
4. Dorian believes that forgiveness for these is impossible.
5. Lord Henry's wife
7. The secret of this is to repeat the follies of it.
9. He advances Sibyl's family 50 pounds.
10. He murders Basil.
11. He shoots the man hiding in the thicket.
13. According to Lord Henry, to be this is to be in harmony with oneself.
14. Author
17. He painted the portrait of Dorian Gray.

The Picture of Dorian Gray Crossword 3 Answer Key

Across
1. Dorian begs Sir Geoffrey not to shoot this.
5. Last name of Sibyl and James
6. It spoiled Sibyl's acting.
8. Dorian claims this can be bought, sold, and bartered away.
10. Person who asks Lord Henry how to become young again
12. Dorian's servants can only identify his body by these.
15. Basil wants to exhibit Dorian's portrait there.
16. It has a huge influence on Dorian's behavior.
18. Dorian goes there after he learns of Sibyl's death.
19. He sees Dorian at the opium house.

Down
1. He has a negative influence on Dorian: Lord ___.
2. He claims Lord Henry is extremely dangerous.
3. Basil sees this in his portrait of Dorian.
4. Dorian believes that forgiveness for these is impossible.
5. Lord Henry's wife
7. The secret of this is to repeat the follies of it.
9. He advances Sibyl's family 50 pounds.
10. He murders Basil.
11. He shoots the man hiding in the thicket.
13. According to Lord Henry, to be this is to be in harmony with oneself.
14. Author
17. He painted the portrait of Dorian Gray.

The Picture of Dorian Gray Crossword 4

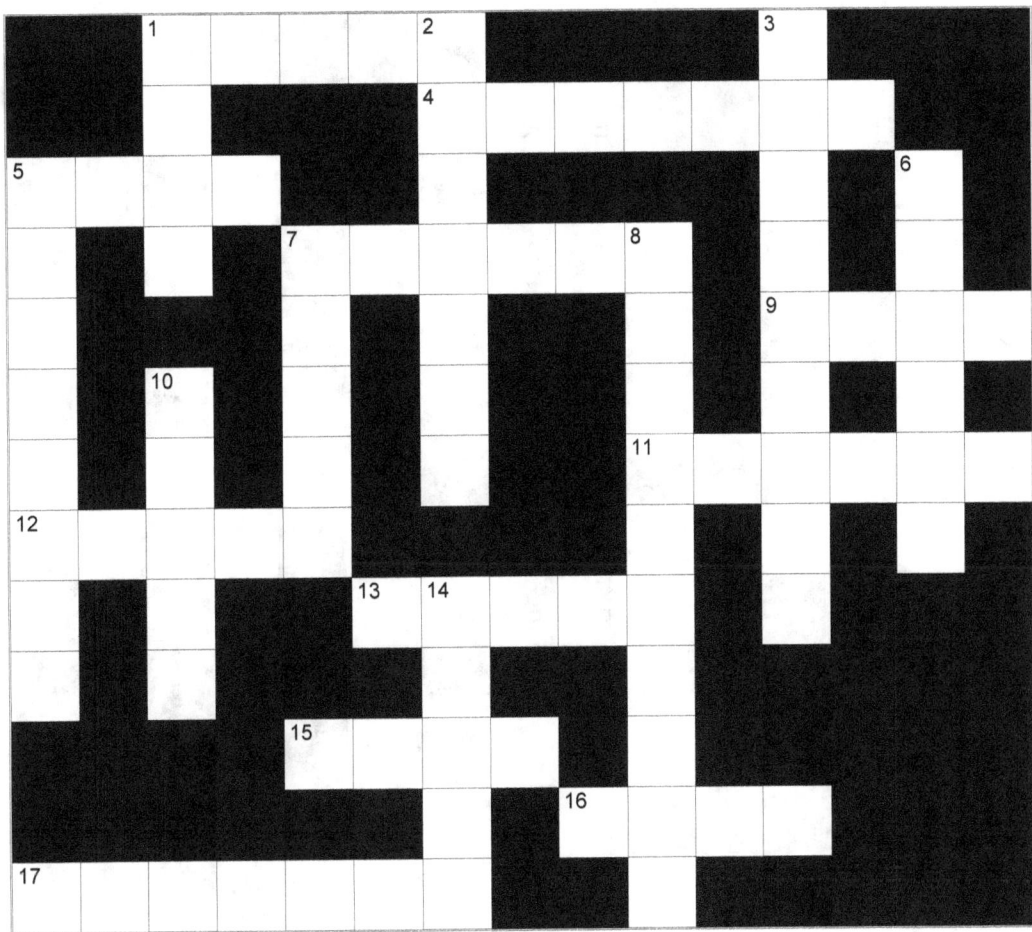

Across
1. Basil sees this in his portrait of Dorian.
4. He claims Lord Henry is extremely dangerous.
5. Last name of Sibyl and James
7. Sibyl's theater role
9. Dorian's housekeeper
11. Sibyl knows Dorian by this 'Charming' name
12. Dorian's servants can only identify his body by these.
13. Dorian goes there after he learns of Sibyl's death.
15. Dorian begs Sir Geoffrey not to shoot this.
16. It has a huge influence on Dorian's behavior.
17. Person who asks Lord Henry how to become young again

Down
1. Dorian believes that forgiveness for these is impossible.
2. It spoiled Sibyl's acting.
3. Lord Henry says these people are colorless and lack individuality.
5. Lord Henry's wife
6. He advances Sibyl's family 50 pounds.
7. He wants to kill Dorian.
8. According to Lord Henry, the only way to get rid of this is to yeild to it.
10. He has a negative influence on Dorian: Lord ___.
14. Basil wants to exhibit Dorian's portrait there.

The Picture of Dorian Gray Crossword 4 Answer Key

Across
1. Basil sees this in his portrait of Dorian.
4. He claims Lord Henry is extremely dangerous.
5. Last name of Sibyl and James
7. Sibyl's theater role
9. Dorian's housekeeper
11. Sibyl knows Dorian by this 'Charming' name
12. Dorian's servants can only identify his body by these.
13. Dorian goes there after he learns of Sibyl's death.
15. Dorian begs Sir Geoffrey not to shoot this.
16. It has a huge influence on Dorian's behavior.
17. Person who asks Lord Henry how to become young again

Down
1. Dorian believes that forgiveness for these is impossible.
2. It spoiled Sibyl's acting.
3. Lord Henry says these people are colorless and lack individuality.
5. Lord Henry's wife
6. He advances Sibyl's family 50 pounds.
7. He wants to kill Dorian.
8. According to Lord Henry, the only way to get rid of this is to yeild to it.
10. He has a negative influence on Dorian: Lord ___.
14. Basil wants to exhibit Dorian's portrait there.

The Picture of Dorian Gray

SHAME	PRINCE	WILDE	REALITY	HENRY
BASIL	TEMPTATION	SYBIL	SINGLETON	PORTRAIT
PARIS	SOUL	FREE SPACE	VANE	SATYR
CLOUSTON	UGLY	BEAUTY	CAMPBELL	LEAF
TELEGRAM	SPHINXES	HETTY	UNSELFISH	DORIAN

The Picture of Dorian Gray

YOUTH	ERSKINE	NARBOROUGH	HARE	DUCHESS
OPERA	CORONER	ISAACS	WAINSCOTING	JULIET
RINGS	SINS	FREE SPACE	VICTORIA	GOOD
FATHER	JAMES	BOOK	DORIAN	UNSELFISH
HETTY	SPHINXES	TELEGRAM	LEAF	CAMPBELL

The Picture of Dorian Gray

CAMPBELL	UNSELFISH	BASIL	SPHINXES	WILDE
PORTRAIT	CRUELTY	YOUTH	PARIS	JAMES
SHAME	DUCHESS	FREE SPACE	WAINSCOTING	VICTORIA
SINGLETON	FATHER	RINGS	REALITY	TELEGRAM
HENRY	PRINCE	SINS	UGLY	NARBOROUGH

The Picture of Dorian Gray

DORIAN	TEMPTATION	SYBIL	HETTY	BOOK
JULIET	GOOD	CORONER	LEAF	BEAUTY
OPERA	BERWICK	FREE SPACE	ISAACS	CLOUSTON
VANE	SATYR	HARE	NARBOROUGH	UGLY
SINS	PRINCE	HENRY	TELEGRAM	REALITY

The Picture of Dorian Gray

RINGS	JULIET	PORTRAIT	OPERA	DORIAN
VANE	JAMES	HETTY	SHAME	CORONER
SINS	REALITY	FREE SPACE	UGLY	SINGLETON
CLOUSTON	BERWICK	SATYR	GOOD	TELEGRAM
PARIS	CAMPBELL	BASIL	ERSKINE	HENRY

The Picture of Dorian Gray

HARE	UNSELFISH	BEAUTY	ISAACS	SPHINXES
FATHER	SYBIL	LEAF	DUCHESS	CRUELTY
YOUTH	WAINSCOTING	FREE SPACE	BOOK	TEMPTATION
PRINCE	SOUL	WILDE	HENRY	ERSKINE
BASIL	CAMPBELL	PARIS	TELEGRAM	GOOD

The Picture of Dorian Gray

PRINCE	SYBIL	HETTY	PARIS	DUCHESS
CAMPBELL	YOUTH	SINGLETON	BASIL	UGLY
CLOUSTON	VICTORIA	FREE SPACE	WILDE	LEAF
BOOK	REALITY	UNSELFISH	ERSKINE	TEMPTATION
HENRY	BEAUTY	SPHINXES	FATHER	CRUELTY

The Picture of Dorian Gray

SOUL	JAMES	PORTRAIT	RINGS	SATYR
JULIET	TELEGRAM	ISAACS	WAINSCOTING	CORONER
BERWICK	HARE	FREE SPACE	SINS	DORIAN
GOOD	SHAME	VANE	CRUELTY	FATHER
SPHINXES	BEAUTY	HENRY	TEMPTATION	ERSKINE

The Picture of Dorian Gray

REALITY	DORIAN	BOOK	BASIL	NARBOROUGH
FATHER	ISAACS	CAMPBELL	BERWICK	DUCHESS
VANE	WAINSCOTING	FREE SPACE	UNSELFISH	LEAF
YOUTH	SPHINXES	SYBIL	UGLY	GOOD
OPERA	SINS	HENRY	CRUELTY	SHAME

The Picture of Dorian Gray

WILDE	SATYR	HARE	JAMES	RINGS
TEMPTATION	PRINCE	BEAUTY	CORONER	TELEGRAM
JULIET	SINGLETON	FREE SPACE	HETTY	PARIS
CLOUSTON	ERSKINE	PORTRAIT	SHAME	CRUELTY
HENRY	SINS	OPERA	GOOD	UGLY

The Picture of Dorian Gray

GOOD	CRUELTY	BOOK	SINS	LEAF
PARIS	REALITY	WILDE	RINGS	YOUTH
DUCHESS	UNSELFISH	FREE SPACE	ERSKINE	ISAACS
NARBOROUGH	TEMPTATION	TELEGRAM	BERWICK	PRINCE
SPHINXES	HENRY	VICTORIA	JULIET	SHAME

The Picture of Dorian Gray

VANE	HARE	CORONER	WAINSCOTING	DORIAN
SOUL	CAMPBELL	BEAUTY	PORTRAIT	FATHER
HETTY	JAMES	FREE SPACE	SINGLETON	SATYR
UGLY	BASIL	CLOUSTON	SHAME	JULIET
VICTORIA	HENRY	SPHINXES	PRINCE	BERWICK

The Picture of Dorian Gray

TELEGRAM	NARBOROUGH	PORTRAIT	BASIL	SATYR
UNSELFISH	WILDE	ERSKINE	CORONER	DORIAN
ISAACS	FATHER	FREE SPACE	JULIET	UGLY
OPERA	SHAME	VICTORIA	HETTY	DUCHESS
BERWICK	SINS	YOUTH	BOOK	GOOD

The Picture of Dorian Gray

CRUELTY	BEAUTY	SINGLETON	PRINCE	CAMPBELL
HENRY	RINGS	REALITY	SPHINXES	SOUL
VANE	PARIS	FREE SPACE	TEMPTATION	LEAF
WAINSCOTING	JAMES	SYBIL	GOOD	BOOK
YOUTH	SINS	BERWICK	DUCHESS	HETTY

The Picture of Dorian Gray

SYBIL	VANE	ISAACS	GOOD	WILDE
RINGS	REALITY	BOOK	VICTORIA	SINGLETON
BEAUTY	CORONER	FREE SPACE	PORTRAIT	TELEGRAM
HETTY	JAMES	LEAF	WAINSCOTING	DUCHESS
ERSKINE	DORIAN	OPERA	SOUL	SHAME

The Picture of Dorian Gray

SPHINXES	UGLY	CRUELTY	NARBOROUGH	SATYR
CAMPBELL	PRINCE	FATHER	TEMPTATION	HENRY
PARIS	UNSELFISH	FREE SPACE	BERWICK	SINS
CLOUSTON	JULIET	YOUTH	SHAME	SOUL
OPERA	DORIAN	ERSKINE	DUCHESS	WAINSCOTING

The Picture of Dorian Gray

SATYR	BERWICK	CRUELTY	DORIAN	OPERA
CORONER	BOOK	SINS	ISAACS	TELEGRAM
GOOD	SPHINXES	FREE SPACE	WILDE	VANE
NARBOROUGH	CAMPBELL	BEAUTY	WAINSCOTING	PARIS
LEAF	PORTRAIT	JAMES	CLOUSTON	FATHER

The Picture of Dorian Gray

HETTY	SHAME	PRINCE	UGLY	SYBIL
YOUTH	HENRY	DUCHESS	VICTORIA	UNSELFISH
JULIET	REALITY	FREE SPACE	ERSKINE	HARE
SOUL	RINGS	BASIL	FATHER	CLOUSTON
JAMES	PORTRAIT	LEAF	PARIS	WAINSCOTING

The Picture of Dorian Gray

SATYR	RINGS	ERSKINE	GOOD	TEMPTATION
FATHER	SINGLETON	CLOUSTON	CORONER	WAINSCOTING
SOUL	UGLY	FREE SPACE	LEAF	HENRY
ISAACS	UNSELFISH	BEAUTY	REALITY	BOOK
SINS	SYBIL	DUCHESS	TELEGRAM	SHAME

The Picture of Dorian Gray

HETTY	HARE	SPHINXES	PORTRAIT	VANE
OPERA	DORIAN	PRINCE	NARBOROUGH	VICTORIA
BERWICK	WILDE	FREE SPACE	JAMES	CRUELTY
YOUTH	CAMPBELL	JULIET	SHAME	TELEGRAM
DUCHESS	SYBIL	SINS	BOOK	REALITY

The Picture of Dorian Gray

CRUELTY	DORIAN	UGLY	CAMPBELL	DUCHESS
HARE	SPHINXES	REALITY	ERSKINE	SINS
SATYR	WAINSCOTING	FREE SPACE	GOOD	VICTORIA
OPERA	SINGLETON	BERWICK	HETTY	RINGS
BEAUTY	SOUL	PARIS	WILDE	YOUTH

The Picture of Dorian Gray

LEAF	JULIET	NARBOROUGH	BOOK	TELEGRAM
SHAME	ISAACS	SYBIL	PRINCE	FATHER
UNSELFISH	TEMPTATION	FREE SPACE	CLOUSTON	BASIL
PORTRAIT	CORONER	HENRY	YOUTH	WILDE
PARIS	SOUL	BEAUTY	RINGS	HETTY

The Picture of Dorian Gray

BOOK	SINGLETON	REALITY	JULIET	HENRY
HETTY	TELEGRAM	TEMPTATION	CRUELTY	CLOUSTON
SATYR	CORONER	FREE SPACE	PRINCE	PARIS
ERSKINE	RINGS	DUCHESS	DORIAN	SOUL
VICTORIA	WAINSCOTING	SPHINXES	SINS	PORTRAIT

The Picture of Dorian Gray

JAMES	HARE	WILDE	UNSELFISH	VANE
BEAUTY	BASIL	CAMPBELL	FATHER	GOOD
UGLY	SHAME	FREE SPACE	OPERA	BERWICK
LEAF	ISAACS	SYBIL	PORTRAIT	SINS
SPHINXES	WAINSCOTING	VICTORIA	SOUL	DORIAN

The Picture of Dorian Gray

JAMES	LEAF	SOUL	SYBIL	HENRY
WAINSCOTING	SINGLETON	ISAACS	RINGS	UGLY
REALITY	FATHER	FREE SPACE	YOUTH	SATYR
UNSELFISH	SINS	CORONER	NARBOROUGH	BEAUTY
GOOD	HARE	CLOUSTON	HETTY	WILDE

The Picture of Dorian Gray

SHAME	CRUELTY	BOOK	OPERA	TELEGRAM
ERSKINE	BASIL	PRINCE	DUCHESS	BERWICK
PARIS	VICTORIA	FREE SPACE	JULIET	VANE
PORTRAIT	SPHINXES	TEMPTATION	WILDE	HETTY
CLOUSTON	HARE	GOOD	BEAUTY	NARBOROUGH

The Picture of Dorian Gray

UGLY	SHAME	CORONER	SATYR	CRUELTY
WILDE	HETTY	ERSKINE	BASIL	BOOK
PARIS	OPERA	FREE SPACE	JULIET	WAINSCOTING
YOUTH	DUCHESS	GOOD	JAMES	TELEGRAM
BERWICK	SPHINXES	FATHER	SYBIL	VANE

The Picture of Dorian Gray

LEAF	RINGS	BEAUTY	HENRY	HARE
CAMPBELL	TEMPTATION	PRINCE	VICTORIA	CLOUSTON
SINGLETON	UNSELFISH	FREE SPACE	SINS	ISAACS
SOUL	DORIAN	PORTRAIT	VANE	SYBIL
FATHER	SPHINXES	BERWICK	TELEGRAM	JAMES

The Picture of Dorian Gray

NARBOROUGH	UGLY	CLOUSTON	LEAF	ISAACS
VANE	JULIET	WAINSCOTING	PARIS	UNSELFISH
SATYR	VICTORIA	FREE SPACE	GOOD	SPHINXES
HETTY	CAMPBELL	DUCHESS	HENRY	PRINCE
ERSKINE	SOUL	JAMES	RINGS	CRUELTY

The Picture of Dorian Gray

BASIL	SINS	TELEGRAM	DORIAN	OPERA
SINGLETON	TEMPTATION	SHAME	YOUTH	SYBIL
CORONER	WILDE	FREE SPACE	HARE	BERWICK
BEAUTY	REALITY	PORTRAIT	CRUELTY	RINGS
JAMES	SOUL	ERSKINE	PRINCE	HENRY

The Picture of Dorian Gray

GOOD	JULIET	WAINSCOTING	PORTRAIT	SINS
TELEGRAM	SATYR	DORIAN	HARE	JAMES
BOOK	RINGS	FREE SPACE	BASIL	YOUTH
CRUELTY	CLOUSTON	WILDE	UGLY	SINGLETON
FATHER	SHAME	VICTORIA	DUCHESS	HENRY

The Picture of Dorian Gray

BEAUTY	ERSKINE	VANE	BERWICK	SYBIL
CAMPBELL	NARBOROUGH	PARIS	SPHINXES	CORONER
ISAACS	LEAF	FREE SPACE	OPERA	TEMPTATION
REALITY	PRINCE	SOUL	HENRY	DUCHESS
VICTORIA	SHAME	FATHER	SINGLETON	UGLY

Dorian Gray Vocabulary Word List

No.	Word	Clue/Definition
1.	ABDICATE	Renounce or relinquish a throne, right, or power
2.	AFFINITY	Natural liking for or attraction to a person, thing, idea, etc.
3.	ANNIHILATES	Destroys completely
4.	ANODYNE	Anything that relieves distress or pain
5.	APHORISMS	Tersely phrased statements of truth or opinion; adages
6.	ASPHODEL	Various plants of the lily family
7.	ATONEMENT	Amends or reparation made for an injury or wrong
8.	BALUSTRADE	Railing at the side of a staircase or balcony
9.	BEATERS	People who rouse or drive game from cover
10.	BRACKEN	Area overgrown with ferns and shrubs
11.	BROUGHAM	Closed four-wheeled carriage with an open driver's seat in the front
12.	CAPRICE	An inclination to change one's mind impulsively
13.	CENSURE	Criticize or reproach harshly
14.	CONJECTURES	Judgments based on inconclusive or incomplete evidence
15.	CONSERVATORY	Greenhouse, usually attached to a dwelling
16.	CORROBORATIVE	Serving to support or to make more certain
17.	CRUCIBLE	Severe, searching test or trial
18.	DEBAUCHERY	Excessive indulgence in sensual pleasures
19.	DEGRADATION	A decline to a lower condition, quality, or level
20.	DESOLATE	Feeling abandoned; forlorn
21.	DISDAIN	Feeling of contempt for anything regarded as unworthy
22.	DISENGAGED	Freed from an engagement, pledge, or obligation
23.	DOWAGERS	Widows who hold property derived from deceased husbands
24.	ELOCUTION	Person's manner of speaking or reading aloud in public
25.	ENNUI	Feeling of utter weariness and discontent resulting from satiety or lack of interest; boredom
26.	ENSCONCED	Settled securely or snugly
27.	ENTHRALL	Captivate or charm
28.	ENTREAT	To ask (a person) earnestly; beseech; implore
29.	EPIGRAM	Concise, clever, often paradoxical statement
30.	ESPIAL	Act of watching, especially in secret
31.	EXPOUND	Set forth or state in detail
32.	FACILE	Easily done, performed, or used
33.	FETID	Having an offensive odor; stinking
34.	FIASCO	Complete and humiliating failure
35.	FLACCID	Soft and limp; not firm; flabby
36.	FOLLIES	Foolishness
37.	FOUNDER	Fill with water and sink
38.	GONDOLA	Long narrow flat-bottomed boat propelled by sculling
39.	GUFFAWED	Laughed heartily and boisterously
40.	HAGGARD	Having a gaunt, wasted, or exhausted appearance, as from prolonged suffering, exertion, or anxiety
41.	HANSOM	Two-wheeled covered carriage with the driver's seat above and behind
42.	HEDONISM	Devotion to pleasure as a way of life
43.	IDOLATROUS	Having excessive or blind adoration, reverence, or devotion
44.	IDYLL	Simple descriptive or narrative piece in verse or prose
45.	IMPASSIVE	Without emotion; apathetic; unmoved
46.	IMPECUNIOSITY	State of having little or no money; penniless; poor
47.	INCARNATION	Assumption of human form or nature
48.	INCORRIGIBLE	Difficult or impossible to control or manage

Dorian Gray Vocabulary Word List

No.	Word	Clue/Definition
49.	INDUCE	To bring about, produce, or cause
50.	INFAMY	Extremly bad reputation
51.	INSOLENCES	Contemptuously rude or impertinent behavior or speech
52.	INTERMINABLE	Seeming to be without an end; endless
53.	INVARIABLY	Without variation or change, in every case
54.	IRRETRIEVABLE	Unable to be recovered or regained
55.	LANGUIDLY	In a manner lacking in spirit or interest; listlessly; indifferently
56.	LIVERIES	Uniforms worn by servants
57.	LUCRATIVE	Producing wealth; profitable
58.	LURID	Gruesome; horrible; revolting
59.	MALADIES	Undesirable conditions or disorders
60.	MEDIOCRITY	State of being ordinary; not outstanding
61.	MISANTHROPE	Hater of humankind
62.	MYRIAD	A very great number of persons or things
63.	OMNIBUS	Vehicle carrying many passengers, used for public transport
64.	ORPHREYS	Ornamental bands or borders, esp. on ecclesiastical vestments
65.	PANEGYRIC	Formal or elaborate praise
66.	PARASOLS	Light, usually small umbrellas carried as protection from the sun
67.	PARODY	Imitate for purposes of ridicule or satire
68.	PATHOS	Feeling of sympathy or pity
69.	PETULANT	Unreasonably irritable or ill-tempered
70.	PHILANTHROPY	Effort or inclination to increase the well-being of humankind
71.	POMPOUS	Characterized by excessive self-esteem or exaggerated dignity
72.	PORTICO	Structure consisting of a roof supported by columns or piers, usually attached to a building
73.	PRATE	Talk excessively and pointlessly; babble
74.	PRECIPICE	Cliff with a vertical or overhanging face
75.	PRESENTIMENT	Feeling of evil to come
76.	PRIG	Self-righteous person who demands pointless conformity
77.	PROCURED	Obtained or gotten by care, effort, or the use of special means
78.	PROFLIGACY	Reckless extravagance
79.	PROTEGE	One whose welfare is promoted by an influential person
80.	PRUDENCE	Caution with regard to practical matters; discretion
81.	QUAY	Landing place constructed along the edge of a body of water
82.	REJOINDER	Answer to a reply; response
83.	REVIVALIST	Person who promotes or holds religious revivals
84.	SANGUINE	Cheerfully optimistic, hopeful, or confident
85.	SATYR	An evil, lascivious man; lecher
86.	SHAMBLED	Walked or went awkwardly; shuffled
87.	SINGED	Burned superficially or slightly; scorched
88.	SMITE	Strike down, injure, or slay
89.	SORDID	Filthy or dirty; foul
90.	STAGNATE	Stop developing, growing, or progressing
91.	TARNISHED	Diminished or became tainted
92.	TAWDRY	Gaudy; showy and cheap
93.	TEDIOUS	Boring, tiring, monotonous, dull
94.	TRIVIAL	Of very little importance or value; insignificant
95.	TURBID	Clouded; opaque; obscured
96.	ULSTER	Long, loose, heavy overcoat
97.	UNADULTERATED	Not mixed with impurities; without qualification
98.	UNCOUTH	Awkward, clumsy, or unmannerly

Dorian Gray Vocabulary Word List

No.	Word	Clue/Definition
99.	VULGARITY	Act or expression that offends good taste or propriety
100	WAINSCOTING	Wood paneling for lining interior walls

Dorian Gray Vocabulary Fill In The Blanks 1

_____ 1. Characterized by excessive self-esteem or exaggerated dignity
_____ 2. Obtained or gotten by care, effort, or the use of special means
_____ 3. Gaudy; showy and cheap
_____ 4. Devotion to pleasure as a way of life
_____ 5. Foolishness
_____ 6. Having an offensive odor; stinking
_____ 7. Set forth or state in detail
_____ 8. Long, loose, heavy overcoat
_____ 9. Long narrow flat-bottomed boat propelled by sculling
_____ 10. Structure consisting of a roof supported by columns or piers, usually attached to a building
_____ 11. Of very little importance or value; insignificant
_____ 12. Concise, clever, often paradoxical statement
_____ 13. To ask (a person) earnestly; beseech; implore
_____ 14. Closed four-wheeled carriage with an open driver's seat in the front
_____ 15. Assumption of human form or nature
_____ 16. Natural liking for or attraction to a person, thing, idea, etc.
_____ 17. Having a gaunt, wasted, or exhausted appearance, as from prolonged suffering, exertion, or anxiety
_____ 18. Not mixed with impurities; without qualification
_____ 19. Judgments based on inconclusive or incomplete evidence
_____ 20. Landing place constructed along the edge of a body of water

Dorian Gray Vocabulary Fill In The Blanks 1 Answer Key

POMPOUS	1. Characterized by excessive self-esteem or exaggerated dignity
PROCURED	2. Obtained or gotten by care, effort, or the use of special means
TAWDRY	3. Gaudy; showy and cheap
HEDONISM	4. Devotion to pleasure as a way of life
FOLLIES	5. Foolishness
FETID	6. Having an offensive odor; stinking
EXPOUND	7. Set forth or state in detail
ULSTER	8. Long, loose, heavy overcoat
GONDOLA	9. Long narrow flat-bottomed boat propelled by sculling
PORTICO	10. Structure consisting of a roof supported by columns or piers, usually attached to a building
TRIVIAL	11. Of very little importance or value; insignificant
EPIGRAM	12. Concise, clever, often paradoxical statement
ENTREAT	13. To ask (a person) earnestly; beseech; implore
BROUGHAM	14. Closed four-wheeled carriage with an open driver's seat in the front
INCARNATION	15. Assumption of human form or nature
AFFINITY	16. Natural liking for or attraction to a person, thing, idea, etc.
HAGGARD	17. Having a gaunt, wasted, or exhausted appearance, as from prolonged suffering, exertion, or anxiety
UNADULTERATED	18. Not mixed with impurities; without qualification
CONJECTURES	19. Judgments based on inconclusive or incomplete evidence
QUAY	20. Landing place constructed along the edge of a body of water

Dorian Gray Vocabulary Fill In The Blanks 2

_____ 1. Amends or reparation made for an injury or wrong

_____ 2. Soft and limp; not firm; flabby

_____ 3. Destroys completely

_____ 4. Feeling of contempt for anything regarded as unworthy

_____ 5. One whose welfare is promoted by an influential person

_____ 6. Without emotion; apathetic; unmoved

_____ 7. Area overgrown with ferns and shrubs

_____ 8. Long narrow flat-bottomed boat propelled by sculling

_____ 9. Renounce or relinquish a throne, right, or power

_____ 10. Wood paneling for lining interior walls

_____ 11. Person who promotes or holds religious revivals

_____ 12. Gaudy; showy and cheap

_____ 13. Serving to support or to make more certain

_____ 14. Feeling abandoned; forlorn

_____ 15. Of very little importance or value; insignificant

_____ 16. Diminished or became tainted

_____ 17. Railing at the side of a staircase or balcony

_____ 18. People who rouse or drive game from cover

_____ 19. Stop developing, growing, or progressing

_____ 20. Unreasonably irritable or ill-tempered

Dorian Gray Vocabulary Fill In The Blanks 2 Answer Key

ATONEMENT	1. Amends or reparation made for an injury or wrong
FLACCID	2. Soft and limp; not firm; flabby
ANNIHILATES	3. Destroys completely
DISDAIN	4. Feeling of contempt for anything regarded as unworthy
PROTEGE	5. One whose welfare is promoted by an influential person
IMPASSIVE	6. Without emotion; apathetic; unmoved
BRACKEN	7. Area overgrown with ferns and shrubs
GONDOLA	8. Long narrow flat-bottomed boat propelled by sculling
ABDICATE	9. Renounce or relinquish a throne, right, or power
WAINSCOTING	10. Wood paneling for lining interior walls
REVIVALIST	11. Person who promotes or holds religious revivals
TAWDRY	12. Gaudy; showy and cheap
CORROBORATIVE	13. Serving to support or to make more certain
DESOLATE	14. Feeling abandoned; forlorn
TRIVIAL	15. Of very little importance or value; insignificant
TARNISHED	16. Diminished or became tainted
BALUSTRADE	17. Railing at the side of a staircase or balcony
BEATERS	18. People who rouse or drive game from cover
STAGNATE	19. Stop developing, growing, or progressing
PETULANT	20. Unreasonably irritable or ill-tempered

Dorian Gray Vocabulary Fill In The Blanks 3

_____ 1. Ornamental bands or borders, esp. on ecclesiastical vestments

_____ 2. Strike down, injure, or slay

_____ 3. Captivate or charm

_____ 4. Landing place constructed along the edge of a body of water

_____ 5. Long narrow flat-bottomed boat propelled by sculling

_____ 6. Natural liking for or attraction to a person, thing, idea, etc.

_____ 7. Person's manner of speaking or reading aloud in public

_____ 8. Imitate for purposes of ridicule or satire

_____ 9. Wood paneling for lining interior walls

_____ 10. People who rouse or drive game from cover

_____ 11. Soft and limp; not firm; flabby

_____ 12. Various plants of the lily family

_____ 13. Feeling of contempt for anything regarded as unworthy

_____ 14. Structure consisting of a roof supported by columns or piers, usually attached to a building

_____ 15. Freed from an engagement, pledge, or obligation

_____ 16. Cliff with a vertical or overhanging face

_____ 17. Seeming to be without an end; endless

_____ 18. Having excessive or blind adoration, reverence, or devotion

_____ 19. Fill with water and sink

_____ 20. Undesirable conditions or disorders

Dorian Gray Vocabulary Fill In The Blanks 3 Answer Key

ORPHREYS	1. Ornamental bands or borders, esp. on ecclesiastical vestments
SMITE	2. Strike down, injure, or slay
ENTHRALL	3. Captivate or charm
QUAY	4. Landing place constructed along the edge of a body of water
GONDOLA	5. Long narrow flat-bottomed boat propelled by sculling
AFFINITY	6. Natural liking for or attraction to a person, thing, idea, etc.
ELOCUTION	7. Person's manner of speaking or reading aloud in public
PARODY	8. Imitate for purposes of ridicule or satire
WAINSCOTING	9. Wood paneling for lining interior walls
BEATERS	10. People who rouse or drive game from cover
FLACCID	11. Soft and limp; not firm; flabby
ASPHODEL	12. Various plants of the lily family
DISDAIN	13. Feeling of contempt for anything regarded as unworthy
PORTICO	14. Structure consisting of a roof supported by columns or piers, usually attached to a building
DISENGAGED	15. Freed from an engagement, pledge, or obligation
PRECIPICE	16. Cliff with a vertical or overhanging face
INTERMINABLE	17. Seeming to be without an end; endless
IDOLATROUS	18. Having excessive or blind adoration, reverence, or devotion
FOUNDER	19. Fill with water and sink
MALADIES	20. Undesirable conditions or disorders

Dorian Gray Vocabulary Fill In The Blanks 4

1. Anything that relieves distress or pain
2. Closed four-wheeled carriage with an open driver's seat in the front
3. Person's manner of speaking or reading aloud in public
4. Self-righteous person who demands pointless conformity
5. Not mixed with impurities; without qualification
6. Ornamental bands or borders, esp. on ecclesiastical vestments
7. Awkward, clumsy, or unmannerly
8. Hater of humankind
9. Renounce or relinquish a throne, right, or power
10. Feeling of utter weariness and discontent resulting from satiety or lack of interest; boredom
11. Stop developing, growing, or progressing
12. Laughed heartily and boisterously
13. Two-wheeled covered carriage with the driver's seat above and behind
14. Feeling of contempt for anything regarded as unworthy
15. Natural liking for or attraction to a person, thing, idea, etc.
16. Gruesome; horrible; revolting
17. Unable to be recovered or regained
18. Concise, clever, often paradoxical statement
19. Severe, searching test or trial
20. Greenhouse, usually attached to a dwelling

Dorian Gray Vocabulary Fill In The Blanks 4 Answer Key

ANODYNE	1. Anything that relieves distress or pain
BROUGHAM	2. Closed four-wheeled carriage with an open driver's seat in the front
ELOCUTION	3. Person's manner of speaking or reading aloud in public
PRIG	4. Self-righteous person who demands pointless conformity
UNADULTERATED	5. Not mixed with impurities; without qualification
ORPHREYS	6. Ornamental bands or borders, esp. on ecclesiastical vestments
UNCOUTH	7. Awkward, clumsy, or unmannerly
MISANTHROPE	8. Hater of humankind
ABDICATE	9. Renounce or relinquish a throne, right, or power
ENNUI	10. Feeling of utter weariness and discontent resulting from satiety or lack of interest; boredom
STAGNATE	11. Stop developing, growing, or progressing
GUFFAWED	12. Laughed heartily and boisterously
HANSOM	13. Two-wheeled covered carriage with the driver's seat above and behind
DISDAIN	14. Feeling of contempt for anything regarded as unworthy
AFFINITY	15. Natural liking for or attraction to a person, thing, idea, etc.
LURID	16. Gruesome; horrible; revolting
IRRETRIEVABLE	17. Unable to be recovered or regained
EPIGRAM	18. Concise, clever, often paradoxical statement
CRUCIBLE	19. Severe, searching test or trial
CONSERVATORY	20. Greenhouse, usually attached to a dwelling

Dorian Gray Vocabulary Matching 1

___ 1. IDOLATROUS   A. Renounce or relinquish a throne, right, or power

___ 2. ATONEMENT   B. Excessive indulgence in sensual pleasures

___ 3. FACILE   C. Easily done, performed, or used

___ 4. ENTREAT   D. Effort or inclination to increase the well-being of humankind

___ 5. INDUCE   E. Assumption of human form or nature

___ 6. APHORISMS   F. Captivate or charm

___ 7. REVIVALIST   G. Difficult or impossible to control or manage

___ 8. CORROBORATIVE   H. Person who promotes or holds religious revivals

___ 9. IRRETRIEVABLE   I. Characterized by excessive self-esteem or exaggerated dignity

___10. PROTEGE   J. Clouded; opaque; obscured

___11. ENNUI   K. To bring about, produce, or cause

___12. ENTHRALL   L. Serving to support or to make more certain

___13. MEDIOCRITY   M. Feeling of utter weariness and discontent resulting from satiety or lack of interest; boredom

___14. LURID   N. Undesirable conditions or disorders

___15. DEGRADATION   O. State of being ordinary; not outstanding

___16. TURBID   P. One whose welfare is promoted by an influential person

___17. DEBAUCHERY   Q. Amends or reparation made for an injury or wrong

___18. INCARNATION   R. Unable to be recovered or regained

___19. ORPHREYS   S. To ask (a person) earnestly; beseech; implore

___20. ASPHODEL   T. A decline to a lower condition, quality, or level

___21. MALADIES   U. Gruesome; horrible; revolting

___22. INCORRIGIBLE   V. Having excessive or blind adoration, reverence, or devotion

___23. PHILANTHROPY   W. Tersely phrased statements of truth or opinion; adages

___24. POMPOUS   X. Various plants of the lily family

___25. ABDICATE   Y. Ornamental bands or borders, esp. on ecclesiastical vestments

Dorian Gray Vocabulary Matching 1 Answer Key

V - 1.	IDOLATROUS	A. Renounce or relinquish a throne, right, or power
Q - 2.	ATONEMENT	B. Excessive indulgence in sensual pleasures
C - 3.	FACILE	C. Easily done, performed, or used
S - 4.	ENTREAT	D. Effort or inclination to increase the well-being of humankind
K - 5.	INDUCE	E. Assumption of human form or nature
W - 6.	APHORISMS	F. Captivate or charm
H - 7.	REVIVALIST	G. Difficult or impossible to control or manage
L - 8.	CORROBORATIVE	H. Person who promotes or holds religious revivals
R - 9.	IRRETRIEVABLE	I. Characterized by excessive self-esteem or exaggerated dignity
P - 10.	PROTEGE	J. Clouded; opaque; obscured
M - 11.	ENNUI	K. To bring about, produce, or cause
F - 12.	ENTHRALL	L. Serving to support or to make more certain
O - 13.	MEDIOCRITY	M. Feeling of utter weariness and discontent resulting from satiety or lack of interest; boredom
U - 14.	LURID	N. Undesirable conditions or disorders
T - 15.	DEGRADATION	O. State of being ordinary; not outstanding
J - 16.	TURBID	P. One whose welfare is promoted by an influential person
B - 17.	DEBAUCHERY	Q. Amends or reparation made for an injury or wrong
E - 18.	INCARNATION	R. Unable to be recovered or regained
Y - 19.	ORPHREYS	S. To ask (a person) earnestly; beseech; implore
X - 20.	ASPHODEL	T. A decline to a lower condition, quality, or level
N - 21.	MALADIES	U. Gruesome; horrible; revolting
G - 22.	INCORRIGIBLE	V. Having excessive or blind adoration, reverence, or devotion
D - 23.	PHILANTHROPY	W. Tersely phrased statements of truth or opinion; adages
I - 24.	POMPOUS	X. Various plants of the lily family
A - 25.	ABDICATE	Y. Ornamental bands or borders, esp. on ecclesiastical vestments

Dorian Gray Vocabulary Matching 2

___ 1. LURID   A. Settled securely or snugly
___ 2. TRIVIAL   B. Without emotion; apathetic; unmoved
___ 3. AFFINITY   C. Devotion to pleasure as a way of life
___ 4. ORPHREYS   D. Severe, searching test or trial
___ 5. ENSCONCED   E. Complete and humiliating failure
___ 6. PETULANT   F. Tersely phrased statements of truth or opinion; adages
___ 7. ATONEMENT   G. Excessive indulgence in sensual pleasures
___ 8. INDUCE   H. Anything that relieves distress or pain
___ 9. IRRETRIEVABLE   I. Amends or reparation made for an injury or wrong
___10. ANODYNE   J. Set forth or state in detail
___11. PANEGYRIC   K. Two-wheeled covered carriage with the driver's seat above and behind
___12. SANGUINE   L. Assumption of human form or nature
___13. ELOCUTION   M. Formal or elaborate praise
___14. CRUCIBLE   N. Structure consisting of a roof supported by columns or piers, usually attached to a building
___15. HANSOM   O. Gruesome; horrible; revolting
___16. EXPOUND   P. Greenhouse, usually attached to a dwelling
___17. TURBID   Q. Unreasonably irritable or ill-tempered
___18. APHORISMS   R. Cheerfully optimistic, hopeful, or confident
___19. CONSERVATORY   S. Unable to be recovered or regained
___20. FIASCO   T. Of very little importance or value; insignificant
___21. PORTICO   U. Natural liking for or attraction to a person, thing, idea, etc.
___22. DEBAUCHERY   V. Ornamental bands or borders, esp. on ecclesiastical vestments
___23. HEDONISM   W. To bring about, produce, or cause
___24. INCARNATION   X. Person's manner of speaking or reading aloud in public
___25. IMPASSIVE   Y. Clouded; opaque; obscured

Dorian Gray Vocabulary Matching 2 Answer Key

O - 1. LURID	A.	Settled securely or snugly
T - 2. TRIVIAL	B.	Without emotion; apathetic; unmoved
U - 3. AFFINITY	C.	Devotion to pleasure as a way of life
V - 4. ORPHREYS	D.	Severe, searching test or trial
A - 5. ENSCONCED	E.	Complete and humiliting failure
Q - 6. PETULANT	F.	Tersely phrased statements of truth or opinion; adages
I - 7. ATONEMENT	G.	Excessive indulgence in sensual pleasures
W - 8. INDUCE	H.	Anything that relieves distress or pain
S - 9. IRRETRIEVABLE	I.	Amends or reparation made for an injury or wrong
H -10. ANODYNE	J.	Set forth or state in detail
M -11. PANEGYRIC	K.	Two-wheeled covered carriage with the driver's seat above and behind
R -12. SANGUINE	L.	Assumption of human form or nature
X -13. ELOCUTION	M.	Formal or elaborate praise
D -14. CRUCIBLE	N.	Structure consisting of a roof supported by columns or piers, usually attached to a building
K -15. HANSOM	O.	Gruesome; horrible; revolting
J -16. EXPOUND	P.	Greenhouse, usually attached to a dwelling
Y -17. TURBID	Q.	Unreasonably irritable or ill-tempered
F -18. APHORISMS	R.	Cheerfully optimistic, hopeful, or confident
P -19. CONSERVATORY	S.	Unable to be recovered or regained
E -20. FIASCO	T.	Of very little importance or value; insignificant
N -21. PORTICO	U.	Natural liking for or attraction to a person, thing, idea, etc.
G -22. DEBAUCHERY	V.	Ornamental bands or borders, esp. on ecclesiastical vestments
C -23. HEDONISM	W.	To bring about, produce, or cause
L -24. INCARNATION	X.	Person's manner of speaking or reading aloud in public
B -25. IMPASSIVE	Y.	Clouded; opaque; obscured

Dorian Gray Vocabulary Matching 3

___ 1. PROTEGE   A. Unreasonably irritable or ill-tempered
___ 2. DESOLATE   B. Self-righteous person who demands pointless conformity
___ 3. CONSERVATORY   C. Clouded; opaque; obscured
___ 4. GONDOLA   D. Devotion to pleasure as a way of life
___ 5. EPIGRAM   E. Gruesome; horrible; revolting
___ 6. INCARNATION   F. Natural liking for or attraction to a person, thing, idea, etc.
___ 7. HEDONISM   G. Assumption of human form or nature
___ 8. PETULANT   H. Characterized by excessive self-esteem or exaggerated dignity
___ 9. TURBID   I. Long narrow flat-bottomed boat propelled by sculling
___10. TRIVIAL   J. Greenhouse, usually attached to a dwelling
___11. PRECIPICE   K. Feeling abandoned; forlorn
___12. PRIG   L. Cliff with a vertical or overhanging face
___13. IMPECUNIOSITY   M. Producing wealth; profitable
___14. ENTREAT   N. Filthy or dirty; foul
___15. SORDID   O. Concise, clever, often paradoxical statement
___16. INCORRIGIBLE   P. Severe, searching test or trial
___17. LUCRATIVE   Q. State of having little or no money; penniless; poor
___18. LURID   R. To ask (a person) earnestly; beseech; implore
___19. AFFINITY   S. Act or expression that offends good taste or propriety
___20. INSOLENCES   T. Stop developing, growing, or progressing
___21. STAGNATE   U. One whose welfare is promoted by an influential person
___22. VULGARITY   V. Difficult or impossible to control or manage
___23. POMPOUS   W. Destroys completely
___24. CRUCIBLE   X. Of very little importance or value; insignificant
___25. ANNIHILATES   Y. Contemptuously rude or impertinent behavior or speech

Dorian Gray Vocabulary Matching 3 Answer Key

U - 1. PROTEGE		A. Unreasonably irritable or ill-tempered
K - 2. DESOLATE		B. Self-righteous person who demands pointless conformity
J - 3. CONSERVATORY		C. Clouded; opaque; obscured
I - 4. GONDOLA		D. Devotion to pleasure as a way of life
O - 5. EPIGRAM		E. Gruesome; horrible; revolting
G - 6. INCARNATION		F. Natural liking for or attraction to a person, thing, idea, etc.
D - 7. HEDONISM		G. Assumption of human form or nature
A - 8. PETULANT		H. Characterized by excessive self-esteem or exaggerated dignity
C - 9. TURBID		I. Long narrow flat-bottomed boat propelled by sculling
X - 10. TRIVIAL		J. Greenhouse, usually attached to a dwelling
L - 11. PRECIPICE		K. Feeling abandoned; forlorn
B - 12. PRIG		L. Cliff with a vertical or overhanging face
Q - 13. IMPECUNIOSITY		M. Producing wealth; profitable
R - 14. ENTREAT		N. Filthy or dirty; foul
N - 15. SORDID		O. Concise, clever, often paradoxical statement
V - 16. INCORRIGIBLE		P. Severe, searching test or trial
M - 17. LUCRATIVE		Q. State of having little or no money; penniless; poor
E - 18. LURID		R. To ask (a person) earnestly; beseech; implore
F - 19. AFFINITY		S. Act or expression that offends good taste or propriety
Y - 20. INSOLENCES		T. Stop developing, growing, or progressing
T - 21. STAGNATE		U. One whose welfare is promoted by an influential person
S - 22. VULGARITY		V. Difficult or impossible to control or manage
H - 23. POMPOUS		W. Destroys completely
P - 24. CRUCIBLE		X. Of very little importance or value; insignificant
W - 25. ANNIHILATES		Y. Contemptuously rude or impertinent behavior or speech

Dorian Gray Vocabulary Matching 4

___ 1. PANEGYRIC   A. Reckless extravagance
___ 2. ATONEMENT   B. Feeling abandoned; forlorn
___ 3. TURBID   C. Feeling of contempt for anything regarded as unworthy
___ 4. HEDONISM   D. Feeling of evil to come
___ 5. EXPOUND   E. Cheerfully optimistic, hopeful, or confident
___ 6. POMPOUS   F. Formal or elaborate praise
___ 7. REVIVALIST   G. Clouded; opaque; obscured
___ 8. ESPIAL   H. Set forth or state in detail
___ 9. INSOLENCES   I. Walked or went awkwardly; shuffled
___10. DESOLATE   J. Various plants of the lily family
___11. PROFLIGACY   K. One whose welfare is promoted by an influential person
___12. SANGUINE   L. A very great number of persons or things
___13. SATYR   M. Filthy or dirty; foul
___14. LIVERIES   N. An evil, lascivious man; lecher
___15. SHAMBLED   O. Uniforms worn by servants
___16. PETULANT   P. Hater of humankind
___17. MYRIAD   Q. Excessive indulgence in sensual pleasures
___18. DISDAIN   R. Person who promotes or holds religious revivals
___19. SORDID   S. Act of watching, especially in secret
___20. PROTEGE   T. Contemptuously rude or impertinent behavior or speech
___21. DEBAUCHERY   U. Characterized by excessive self-esteem or exaggerated dignity
___22. PRESENTIMENT   V. Devotion to pleasure as a way of life
___23. MISANTHROPE   W. Amends or reparation made for an injury or wrong
___24. ASPHODEL   X. Unreasonably irritable or ill-tempered
___25. BROUGHAM   Y. Closed four-wheeled carriage with an open driver's seat in the front

Dorian Gray Vocabulary Matching 4 Answer Key

F - 1. PANEGYRIC	A.	Reckless extravagance
W - 2. ATONEMENT	B.	Feeling abandoned; forlorn
G - 3. TURBID	C.	Feeling of contempt for anything regarded as unworthy
V - 4. HEDONISM	D.	Feeling of evil to come
H - 5. EXPOUND	E.	Cheerfully optimistic, hopeful, or confident
U - 6. POMPOUS	F.	Formal or elaborate praise
R - 7. REVIVALIST	G.	Clouded; opaque; obscured
S - 8. ESPIAL	H.	Set forth or state in detail
T - 9. INSOLENCES	I.	Walked or went awkwardly; shuffled
B - 10. DESOLATE	J.	Various plants of the lily family
A - 11. PROFLIGACY	K.	One whose welfare is promoted by an influential person
E - 12. SANGUINE	L.	A very great number of persons or things
N - 13. SATYR	M.	Filthy or dirty; foul
O - 14. LIVERIES	N.	An evil, lascivious man; lecher
I - 15. SHAMBLED	O.	Uniforms worn by servants
X - 16. PETULANT	P.	Hater of humankind
L - 17. MYRIAD	Q.	Excessive indulgence in sensual pleasures
C - 18. DISDAIN	R.	Person who promotes or holds religious revivals
M - 19. SORDID	S.	Act of watching, especially in secret
K - 20. PROTEGE	T.	Contemptuously rude or impertinent behavior or speech
Q - 21. DEBAUCHERY	U.	Characterized by excessive self-esteem or exaggerated dignity
D - 22. PRESENTIMENT	V.	Devotion to pleasure as a way of life
P - 23. MISANTHROPE	W.	Amends or reparation made for an injury or wrong
J - 24. ASPHODEL	X.	Unreasonably irritable or ill-tempered
Y - 25. BROUGHAM	Y.	Closed four-wheeled carriage with an open driver's seat in the front

Dorian Gray Vocabulary Magic Squares 1

Match the definition with the vocabulary word. Put your answers in the magic squares below. When your answers are correct, all columns and rows will add to the same number.

A. INCARNATION
B. QUAY
C. ENTHRALL
D. GUFFAWED
E. TURBID
F. FETID
G. PORTICO
H. INTERMINABLE
I. BRACKEN
J. SHAMBLED
K. BALUSTRADE
L. ENSCONCED
M. PRATE
N. REVIVALIST
O. MEDIOCRITY
P. SATYR

1. Landing place constructed along the edge of a body of water
2. Structure consisting of a roof supported by columns or piers, usually attached to a building
3. Railing at the side of a staircase or balcony
4. Person who promotes or holds religious revivals
5. Talk excessively and pointlessly; babble
6. Settled securely or snugly
7. Seeming to be without an end; endless
8. Assumption of human form or nature
9. An evil, lascivious man; lecher
10. Area overgrown with ferns and shrubs
11. Clouded; opaque; obscured
12. Laughed heartily and boisterously
13. Captivate or charm
14. Having an offensive odor; stinking
15. Walked or went awkwardly; shuffled
16. State of being ordinary; not outstanding

A=	B=	C=	D=
E=	F=	G=	H=
I=	J=	K=	L=
M=	N=	O=	P=

Dorian Gray Vocabulary Magic Squares 1 Answer Key

Match the definition with the vocabulary word. Put your answers in the magic squares below. When your answers are correct, all columns and rows will add to the same number.

A. INCARNATION
B. QUAY
C. ENTHRALL
D. GUFFAWED
E. TURBID
F. FETID
G. PORTICO
H. INTERMINABLE
I. BRACKEN
J. SHAMBLED
K. BALUSTRADE
L. ENSCONCED
M. PRATE
N. REVIVALIST
O. MEDIOCRITY
P. SATYR

1. Landing place constructed along the edge of a body of water
2. Structure consisting of a roof supported by columns or piers, usually attached to a building
3. Railing at the side of a staircase or balcony
4. Person who promotes or holds religious revivals
5. Talk excessively and pointlessly; babble
6. Settled securely or snugly
7. Seeming to be without an end; endless
8. Assumption of human form or nature
9. An evil, lascivious man; lecher
10. Area overgrown with ferns and shrubs
11. Clouded; opaque; obscured
12. Laughed heartily and boisterously
13. Captivate or charm
14. Having an offensive odor; stinking
15. Walked or went awkwardly; shuffled
16. State of being ordinary; not outstanding

A=8	B=1	C=13	D=12
E=11	F=14	G=2	H=7
I=10	J=15	K=3	L=6
M=5	N=4	O=16	P=9

Dorian Gray Vocabulary Magic Squares 2

Match the definition with the vocabulary word. Put your answers in the magic squares below. When your answers are correct, all columns and rows will add to the same number.

A. INVARIABLY
B. PROFLIGACY
C. MISANTHROPE
D. SORDID
E. IDYLL
F. IMPECUNIOSITY
G. INSOLENCES
H. ELOCUTION
I. PRECIPICE
J. FETID
K. FOUNDER
L. TEDIOUS
M. INTERMINABLE
N. VULGARITY
O. LUCRATIVE
P. INDUCE

1. Seeming to be without an end; endless
2. State of having little or no money; penniless; poor
3. Person's manner of speaking or reading aloud in public
4. Producing wealth; profitable
5. Boring, tiring, monotonous, dull
6. Hater of humankind
7. Without variation or change, in every case
8. Having an offensive odor; stinking
9. Fill with water and sink
10. Filthy or dirty; foul
11. Reckless extravagance
12. Cliff with a vertical or overhanging face
13. Act or expression that offends good taste or propriety
14. Simple descriptive or narrative piece in verse or prose
15. Contemptuously rude or impertinent behavior or speech
16. To bring about, produce, or cause

A=	B=	C=	D=
E=	F=	G=	H=
I=	J=	K=	L=
M=	N=	O=	P=

Dorian Gray Vocabulary Magic Squares 2 Answer Key

Match the definition with the vocabulary word. Put your answers in the magic squares below. When your answers are correct, all columns and rows will add to the same number.

A. INVARIABLY
B. PROFLIGACY
C. MISANTHROPE
D. SORDID
E. IDYLL
F. IMPECUNIOSITY
G. INSOLENCES
H. ELOCUTION
I. PRECIPICE
J. FETID
K. FOUNDER
L. TEDIOUS
M. INTERMINABLE
N. VULGARITY
O. LUCRATIVE
P. INDUCE

1. Seeming to be without an end; endless
2. State of having little or no money; penniless; poor
3. Person's manner of speaking or reading aloud in public
4. Producing wealth; profitable
5. Boring, tiring, monotonous, dull
6. Hater of humankind
7. Without variation or change, in every case
8. Having an offensive odor; stinking
9. Fill with water and sink
10. Filthy or dirty; foul
11. Reckless extravagance
12. Cliff with a vertical or overhanging face
13. Act or expression that offends good taste or propriety
14. Simple descriptive or narrative piece in verse or prose
15. Contemptuously rude or impertinent behavior or speech
16. To bring about, produce, or cause

A=7	B=11	C=6	D=10
E=14	F=2	G=15	H=3
I=12	J=8	K=9	L=5
M=1	N=13	O=4	P=16

Dorian Gray Vocabulary Magic Squares 3

Match the definition with the vocabulary word. Put your answers in the magic squares below. When your answers are correct, all columns and rows will add to the same number.

A. REVIVALIST
B. FIASCO
C. HEDONISM
D. INCORRIGIBLE
E. DEGRADATION
F. SHAMBLED
G. ESPIAL
H. PROCURED
I. INVARIABLY
J. CONJECTURES
K. INFAMY
L. PORTICO
M. SMITE
N. ENSCONCED
O. IDOLATROUS
P. DOWAGERS

1. Having excessive or blind adoration, reverence, or devotion
2. Difficult or impossible to control or manage
3. Judgments based on inconclusive or incomplete evidence
4. A decline to a lower condition, quality, or level
5. Without variation or change, in every case
6. Walked or went awkwardly; shuffled
7. Widows who hold property derived from deceased husbands
8. Devotion to pleasure as a way of life
9. Obtained or gotten by care, effort, or the use of special means
10. Extremly bad reputation
11. Person who promotes or holds religious revivals
12. Settled securely or snugly
13. Complete and humiliting failure
14. Strike down, injure, or slay
15. Act of watching, especially in secret
16. Structure consisting of a roof supported by columns or piers, usually attached to a attached to a building

A=	B=	C=	D=
E=	F=	G=	H=
I=	J=	K=	L=
M=	N=	O=	P=

Dorian Gray Vocabulary Magic Squares 3 Answer Key

Match the definition with the vocabulary word. Put your answers in the magic squares below. When your answers are correct, all columns and rows will add to the same number.

A. REVIVALIST
B. FIASCO
C. HEDONISM
D. INCORRIGIBLE
E. DEGRADATION
F. SHAMBLED
G. ESPIAL
H. PROCURED
I. INVARIABLY
J. CONJECTURES
K. INFAMY
L. PORTICO
M. SMITE
N. ENSCONCED
O. IDOLATROUS
P. DOWAGERS

1. Having excessive or blind adoration, reverence, or devotion
2. Difficult or impossible to control or manage
3. Judgments based on inconclusive or incomplete evidence
4. A decline to a lower condition, quality, or level
5. Without variation or change, in every case
6. Walked or went awkwardly; shuffled
7. Widows who hold property derived from deceased husbands
8. Devotion to pleasure as a way of life
9. Obtained or gotten by care, effort, or the use of special means
10. Extremly bad reputation
11. Person who promotes or holds religious revivals
12. Settled securely or snugly
13. Complete and humiliting failure
14. Strike down, injure, or slay
15. Act of watching, especially in secret
16. Structure consisting of a roof supported by columns or piers, usually attached to a attached to a building

A=11	B=13	C=8	D=2
E=4	F=6	G=15	H=9
I=5	J=3	K=10	L=16
M=14	N=12	O=1	P=7

Dorian Gray Vocabulary Magic Squares 4

Match the definition with the vocabulary word. Put your answers in the magic squares below. When your answers are correct, all columns and rows will add to the same number.

A. PORTICO
B. PRESENTIMENT
C. BRACKEN
D. FOLLIES
E. MALADIES
F. ENTREAT
G. ENNUI
H. ANODYNE
I. TAWDRY
J. ABDICATE
K. FOUNDER
L. GONDOLA
M. IMPECUNIOSITY
N. ENSCONCED
O. ULSTER
P. BALUSTRADE

1. Anything that relieves distress or pain
2. State of having little or no money; penniless; poor
3. Feeling of evil to come
4. Fill with water and sink
5. Renounce or relinquish a throne, right, or power
6. Area overgrown with ferns and shrubs
7. Railing at the side of a staircase or balcony
8. Undesirable conditions or disorders
9. Long, loose, heavy overcoat
10. To ask (a person) earnestly; beseech; implore
11. Gaudy; showy and cheap
12. Foolishness
13. Structure consisting of a roof supported by columns or piers, usually attached to a building
14. Long narrow flat-bottomed boat propelled by sculling
15. Feeling of utter weariness and discontent resulting from satiety or lack of interest; boredom
16. Settled securely or snugly

A=	B=	C=	D=
E=	F=	G=	H=
I=	J=	K=	L=
M=	N=	O=	P=

Dorian Gray Vocabulary Magic Squares 4 Answer Key

Match the definition with the vocabulary word. Put your answers in the magic squares below. When your answers are correct, all columns and rows will add to the same number.

A. PORTICO
B. PRESENTIMENT
C. BRACKEN
D. FOLLIES
E. MALADIES
F. ENTREAT
G. ENNUI
H. ANODYNE
I. TAWDRY
J. ABDICATE
K. FOUNDER
L. GONDOLA
M. IMPECUNIOSITY
N. ENSCONCED
O. ULSTER
P. BALUSTRADE

1. Anything that relieves distress or pain
2. State of having little or no money; penniless; poor
3. Feeling of evil to come
4. Fill with water and sink
5. Renounce or relinquish a throne, right, or power
6. Area overgrown with ferns and shrubs
7. Railing at the side of a staircase or balcony
8. Undesirable conditions or disorders
9. Long, loose, heavy overcoat
10. To ask (a person) earnestly; beseech; implore
11. Gaudy; showy and cheap
12. Foolishness
13. Structure consisting of a roof supported by columns or piers, usually attached to a building
14. Long narrow flat-bottomed boat propelled by sculling
15. Feeling of utter weariness and discontent resulting from satiety or lack of interest; boredom
16. Settled securely or snugly

A=13	B=3	C=6	D=12
E=8	F=10	G=15	H=1
I=11	J=5	K=4	L=14
M=2	N=16	O=9	P=7

Dorian Gray Vocabulary Juggle Letters 1

1. RNKBECA = 1. _____
   Area overgrown with ferns and shrubs

2. DILYL = 2. _____
   Simple descriptive or narrative piece in verse or prose

3. ABEENMLIITNR = 3. _____
   Seeming to be without an end; endless

4. LFECIA = 4. _____
   Easily done, performed, or used

5. DCIBEAAT = 5. _____
   Renounce or relinquish a throne, right, or power

6. RYAOPD = 6. _____
   Imitate for purposes of ridicule or satire

7. NCEEOSDCN = 7. _____
   Settled securely or snugly

8. GGAAHRD = 8. _____
   Having a gaunt, wasted, or exhausted appearance, as from prolonged suffering, exertion, or anxiety

9. AYWRDT = 9. _____
   Gaudy; showy and cheap

10. DSADIIN =10. _____
    Feeling of contempt for anything regarded as unworthy

11. TRPCOOI =11. _____
    Structure consisting of a roof supported by columns or piers, usually attached to a building

12. PPSOMUO =12. _____
    Characterized by excessive self-esteem or exaggerated dignity

13. RDYMAI =13. _____
    A very great number of persons or things

14. ITOUDES =14. _____
    Boring, tiring, monotonous, dull

Dorian Gray Vocabulary Juggle Letters 1 Answer Key

1. RNKBECA = 1. BRACKEN
   Area overgrown with ferns and shrubs

2. DILYL = 2. IDYLL
   Simple descriptive or narrative piece in verse or prose

3. ABEENMLIITNR = 3. INTERMINABLE
   Seeming to be without an end; endless

4. LFECIA = 4. FACILE
   Easily done, performed, or used

5. DCIBEAAT = 5. ABDICATE
   Renounce or relinquish a throne, right, or power

6. RYAOPD = 6. PARODY
   Imitate for purposes of ridicule or satire

7. NCEEOSDCN = 7. ENSCONCED
   Settled securely or snugly

8. GGAAHRD = 8. HAGGARD
   Having a gaunt, wasted, or exhausted appearance, as from prolonged suffering, exertion, or anxiety

9. AYWRDT = 9. TAWDRY
   Gaudy; showy and cheap

10. DSADIIN = 10. DISDAIN
    Feeling of contempt for anything regarded as unworthy

11. TRPCOOI = 11. PORTICO
    Structure consisting of a roof supported by columns or piers, usually attached to a building

12. PPSOMUO = 12. POMPOUS
    Characterized by excessive self-esteem or exaggerated dignity

13. RDYMAI = 13. MYRIAD
    A very great number of persons or things

14. ITOUDES = 14. TEDIOUS
    Boring, tiring, monotonous, dull

Dorian Gray Vocabulary Juggle Letters 2

1. GMUOAHBR = 1. _____
   Closed four-wheeled carriage with an open driver's seat in the front

2. LBANIAYVIR = 2. _____
   Without variation or change, in every case

3. LETURS = 3. _____
   Long, loose, heavy overcoat

4. VAIURTGLY = 4. _____
   Act or expression that offends good taste or propriety

5. ERAADSBUTL = 5. _____
   Railing at the side of a staircase or balcony

6. ARTENTE = 6. _____
   To ask (a person) earnestly; beseech; implore

7. TLSDUOIAOR = 7. _____
   Having excessive or blind adoration, reverence, or devotion

8. AUYQ = 8. _____
   Landing place constructed along the edge of a body of water

9. LRNNABIIMEET = 9. _____
   Seeming to be without an end; endless

10. GMIEPRA = 10. _____
    Concise, clever, often paradoxical statement

11. OANMSH = 11. _____
    Two-wheeled covered carriage with the driver's seat above and behind

12. INSAAHLINTE = 12. _____
    Destroys completely

13. SEALIP = 13. _____
    Act of watching, especially in secret

14. ALFDCIC = 14. _____
    Soft and limp; not firm; flabby

Dorian Gray Vocabulary Juggle Letters 2 Answer Key

1. GMUOAHBR = 1. BROUGHAM
Closed four-wheeled carriage with an open driver's seat in the front

2. LBANIAYVIR = 2. INVARIABLY
Without variation or change, in every case

3. LETURS = 3. ULSTER
Long, loose, heavy overcoat

4. VAIURTGLY = 4. VULGARITY
Act or expression that offends good taste or propriety

5. ERAADSBUTL = 5. BALUSTRADE
Railing at the side of a staircase or balcony

6. ARTENTE = 6. ENTREAT
To ask (a person) earnestly; beseech; implore

7. TLSDUOIAOR = 7. IDOLATROUS
Having excessive or blind adoration, reverence, or devotion

8. AUYQ = 8. QUAY
Landing place constructed along the edge of a body of water

9. LRNNABIIMEET = 9. INTERMINABLE
Seeming to be without an end, endless

10. GMIEPRA = 10. EPIGRAM
Concise, clever, often paradoxical statement

11. OANMSH = 11. HANSOM
Two-wheeled covered carriage with the driver's seat above and behind

12. INSAAHLINTE = 12. ANNIHILATES
Destroys completely

13. SEALIP = 13. ESPIAL
Act of watching, especially in secret

14. ALFDCIC = 14. FLACCID
Soft and limp; not firm; flabby

Dorian Gray Vocabulary Juggle Letters 3

1. NEEISREPTNTM = 1. _____
Feeling of evil to come

2. PIAGRME = 2. _____
Concise, clever, often paradoxical statement

3. ATPTLENU = 3. _____
Unreasonably irritable or ill-tempered

4. YHOEPSRR = 4. _____
Ornamental bands or borders, esp. on ecclesiastical vestments

5. LDLYI = 5. _____
Simple descriptive or narrative piece in verse or prose

6. RBTUDI = 6. _____
Clouded; opaque; obscured

7. AHRUMBOG = 7. _____
Closed four-wheeled carriage with an open driver's seat in the front

8. IIANNGSWTOC = 8. _____
Wood paneling for lining interior walls

9. CUNTJREOESC = 9. _____
Judgments based on inconclusive or incomplete evidence

10. NGSENUAI = 10. _____
Cheerfully optimistic, hopeful, or confident

11. IEDFT = 11. _____
Having an offensive odor; stinking

12. USOMNIB = 12. _____
Vehicle carrying many passengers, used for public transport

13. ETONNETMA = 13. _____
Amends or reparation made for an injury or wrong

14. REBTSEA = 14. _____
People who rouse or drive game from cover

Dorian Gray Vocabulary Juggle Letters 3 Answer Key

1. NEEISREPTNTM = 1. PRESENTIMENT
   Feeling of evil to come

2. PIAGRME = 2. EPIGRAM
   Concise, clever, often paradoxical statement

3. ATPTLENU = 3. PETULANT
   Unreasonably irritable or ill-tempered

4. YHOEPSRR = 4. ORPHREYS
   Ornamental bands or borders, esp. on ecclesiastical vestments

5. LDLYI = 5. IDYLL
   Simple descriptive or narrative piece in verse or prose

6. RBTUDI = 6. TURBID
   Clouded; opaque; obscured

7. AHRUMBOG = 7. BROUGHAM
   Closed four-wheeled carriage with an open driver's seat in the front

8. IIANNGSWTOC = 8. WAINSCOTING
   Wood paneling for lining interior walls

9. CUNTJREOESC = 9. CONJECTURES
   Judgments based on inconclusive or incomplete evidence

10. NGSENUAI = 10. SANGUINE
    Cheerfully optimistic, hopeful, or confident

11. IEDFT = 11. FETID
    Having an offensive odor; stinking

12. USOMNIB = 12. OMNIBUS
    Vehicle carrying many passengers, used for public transport

13. ETONNETMA = 13. ATONEMENT
    Amends or reparation made for an injury or wrong

14. REBTSEA = 14. BEATERS
    People who rouse or drive game from cover

Dorian Gray Vocabulary Juggle Letters 4

1. RSTAY = 1. _____
An evil, lascivious man; lecher

2. MHIODNSE = 2. _____
Devotion to pleasure as a way of life

3. IUTEONCLO = 3. _____
Person's manner of speaking or reading aloud in public

4. AOINCNRATNI = 4. _____
Assumption of human form or nature

5. OUNTHCU = 5. _____
Awkward, clumsy, or unmannerly

6. URHEYDCAEB = 6. _____
Excessive indulgence in sensual pleasures

7. LBINAINRETME = 7. _____
Seeming to be without an end; endless

8. ESOAEDLT = 8. _____
Feeling abandoned; forlorn

9. EIUCVTRLA = 9. _____
Producing wealth; profitable

10. NIMOAETHPRS =10. _____
Hater of humankind

11. EUATEDATRNUDL =11. _____
Not mixed with impurities; without qualification

12. IRUDL =12. _____
Gruesome; horrible; revolting

13. OCELNSEINS =13. _____
Contemptuously rude or impertinent behavior or speech

14. RIYAMD =14. _____
A very great number of persons or things

Dorian Gray Vocabulary Juggle Letters 4 Answer Key

1. RSTAY = 1. SATYR
   An evil, lascivious man; lecher

2. MHIODNSE = 2. HEDONISM
   Devotion to pleasure as a way of life

3. IUTEONCLO = 3. ELOCUTION
   Person's manner of speaking or reading aloud in public

4. AOINCNRATNI = 4. INCARNATION
   Assumption of human form or nature

5. OUNTHCU = 5. UNCOUTH
   Awkward, clumsy, or unmannerly

6. URHEYDCAEB = 6. DEBAUCHERY
   Excessive indulgence in sensual pleasures

7. LBINAINRETME = 7. INTERMINABLE
   Seeming to be without an end; endless

8. ESOAEDLT = 8. DESOLATE
   Feeling abandoned; forlorn

9. EIUCVTRLA = 9. LUCRATIVE
   Producing wealth; profitable

10. NIMOAETHPRS = 10. MISANTHROPE
    Hater of humankind

11. EUATEDATRNUDL = 11. UNADULTERATED
    Not mixed with impurities; without qualification

12. IRUDL = 12. LURID
    Gruesome; horrible; revolting

13. OCELNSEINS = 13. INSOLENCES
    Contemptuously rude or impertinent behavior or speech

14. RIYAMD = 14. MYRIAD
    A very great number of persons or things

Dorian Gray Vocabulary Word Search 1

```
R T A W D R Y H E W P O M P O U S
N E N T R E A T N G Q A A L G W B
L P V U L G A R I T Y D T R R E A
U A R I G Q W R U N E E O H A V S
R R P A V Z P Y G C F T N T O I P
I O R T A Y Z N P D A E R C S H
D D O P E E L O A E L R M P I S O
C Y M R Q C C I S M S E E Y T A D
R F N K P S I O S I A T N D R P E
U O I M N H L P U T U L T Y O M L
C U B E Q A R N I L I U A K P I L
I N U F T U N E A C J D S D P X A
B D S E Y E A N Y N E A Y M I C I
L E H T S A T Y R S N N D L I E P
E R J I E X P O U N D U G Q L T S
S O R D I D P A N E G Y R I C F E
```

Act of watching, especially in secret (6)
Act or expression that offends good taste or propriety (9)
Amends or reparation made for an injury or wrong (9)
An evil, lascivious man; lecher (5)
Characterized by excessive self-esteem or exaggerated dignity (7)
Cheerfully optimistic, hopeful, or confident (8)
Cliff with a vertical or overhanging face (9)
Extremly bad reputation (6)
Feeling abandoned; forlorn (8)
Feeling of sympathy or pity (6)
Feeling of utter weariness and discontent resulting from satiety or lack of interest; boredom (5)
Fill with water and sink (7)
Filthy or dirty; foul (6)
Formal or elaborate praise (9)
Gaudy; showy and cheap (6)
Gruesome; horrible; revolting (5)
Having a gaunt, wasted, or exhausted appearance, as from prolonged suffering, exertion, or anxiety
Having an offensive odor; stinking (5)
Imitate for purposes of ridicule or satire (6)
Landing place constructed along the edge of a body of water (4)

Not mixed with impurities; without qualification (13)
Ornamental bands or borders, esp. on ecclesiastical vestments (8)
People who rouse or drive game from cover (7)
Person who promotes or holds religious revivals (10)
Self-righteous person who demands pointless conformity (4)
Set forth or state in detail (7)
Settled securely or snugly (9)
Severe, searching test or trial (8)
Simple descriptive or narrative piece in verse or prose (5)
Strike down, injure, or slay (5)
Structure consisting of a roof supported by columns or piers, usually attached to a building (7)
Talk excessively and pointlessly; babble (5)
To ask (a person) earnestly; beseech; implore (7)
Undesirable conditions or disorders (8)
Unreasonably irritable or ill-tempered (8)
Various plants of the lily family (8)
Vehicle carrying many passengers, used for public transport (7)
Without emotion; apathetic; unmoved (9)

Dorian Gray Vocabulary Word Search 1 Answer Key

- Act of watching, especially in secret (6)
- Act or expression that offends good taste or propriety (9)
- Amends or reparation made for an injury or wrong (9)
- An evil, lascivious man; lecher (5)
- Characterized by excessive self-esteem or exaggerated dignity (7)
- Cheerfully optimistic, hopeful, or confident (8)
- Cliff with a vertical or overhanging face (9)
- Extremly bad reputation (6)
- Feeling abandoned; forlorn (8)
- Feeling of sympathy or pity (6)
- Feeling of utter weariness and discontent resulting from satiety or lack of interest; boredom (5)
- Fill with water and sink (7)
- Filthy or dirty; foul (6)
- Formal or elaborate praise (9)
- Gaudy; showy and cheap (6)
- Gruesome; horrible; revolting (5)
- Having a gaunt, wasted, or exhausted appearance, as from prolonged suffering, exertion, or anxiety
- Having an offensive odor; stinking (5)
- Imitate for purposes of ridicule or satire (6)
- Landing place constructed along the edge of a body of water (4)
- Not mixed with impurities; without qualification (13)
- Ornamental bands or borders, esp. on ecclesiastical vestments (8)
- People who rouse or drive game from cover (7)
- Person who promotes or holds religious revivals (10)
- Self-righteous person who demands pointless conformity (4)
- Set forth or state in detail (7)
- Settled securely or snugly (9)
- Severe, searching test or trial (8)
- Simple descriptive or narrative piece in verse or prose (5)
- Strike down, injure, or slay (5)
- Structure consisting of a roof supported by columns or piers, usually attached to a building (7)
- Talk excessively and pointlessly; babble (5)
- To ask (a person) earnestly; beseech; implore (7)
- Undesirable conditions or disorders (8)
- Unreasonably irritable or ill-tempered (8)
- Various plants of the lily family (8)
- Vehicle carrying many passengers, used for public transport (7)
- Without emotion; apathetic; unmoved (9)

Dorian Gray Vocabulary Word Search 2

```
E  N  S  C  O  N  C  E  D  N  U  O  P  X  E  D  P
C  P  O  T  K  R  D  I  S  D  A  I  N  S  G  A  O
I  N  R  M  A  S  P  H  O  D  E  L  G  E  S  I  M
R  K  D  A  N  G  I  H  E  C  I  P  I  C  E  R  P
P  R  I  G  T  I  N  N  R  D  C  Q  X  N  I  Y  O
A  F  D  A  N  E  B  A  D  E  O  S  Y  E  D  M  U
C  F  E  N  N  U  I  U  T  U  Y  N  K  L  A  U  S
B  N  S  T  V  O  D  D  S  E  C  S  I  O  L  H  B
Q  K  P  C  I  I  D  B  E  A  T  E  R  S  A  S  D
F  Q  I  M  R  D  X  Y  P  T  D  Q  T  N  M  R  E
L  P  A  U  L  K  Y  M  N  A  D  E  S  I  A  E  L
F  O  L  L  I  E  S  Y  J  E  R  O  N  G  T  G  B
S  A  T  Y  R  M  A  W  G  R  M  O  G  H  X  A  M
L  L  Y  D  I  U  H  N  M  T  W  A  D  K  T  W  A
G  C  B  T  Q  Y  I  N  M  N  H  J  G  Y  Z  O  H
V  Z  E  R  U  S  N  E  C  E  T  U  R  B  I  D  S
```

A very great number of persons or things (6)
Act of watching, especially in secret (6)
An evil, lascivious man; lecher (5)
An inclination to change one's mind impulsively (7)
Anything that relieves distress or pain (7)
Burned superficially or slightly; scorched (6)
Characterized by excessive self-esteem or exaggerated dignity (7)
Cliff with a vertical or overhanging face (9)
Clouded; opaque; obscured (6)
Contemptuously rude or impertinent behavior or speech (10)
Criticize or reproach harshly (7)
Devotion to pleasure as a way of life (8)
Feeling of contempt for anything regarded as unworthy (7)
Feeling of utter weariness and discontent resulting from satiety or lack of interest; boredom (5)
Filthy or dirty; foul (6)
Foolishness (7)
Gruesome; horrible; revolting (5)
Having a gaunt, wasted, or exhausted appearance, as from prolonged suffering, exertion, or anxiety
Having an offensive odor; stinking (5)
Imitate for purposes of ridicule or satire (6)

Landing place constructed along the edge of a body of water (4)
Long, loose, heavy overcoat (6)
Ornamental bands or borders, esp. on ecclesiastical vestments (8)
People who rouse or drive game from cover (7)
Self-righteous person who demands pointless conformity (4)
Set forth or state in detail (7)
Settled securely or snugly (9)
Simple descriptive or narrative piece in verse or prose (5)
Stop developing, growing, or progressing (8)
Strike down, injure, or slay (5)
Talk excessively and pointlessly; babble (5)
To ask (a person) earnestly; beseech; implore (7)
To bring about, produce, or cause (6)
Two-wheeled covered carriage with the driver's seat above and behind (6)
Undesirable conditions or disorders (8)
Various plants of the lily family (8)
Vehicle carrying many passengers, used for public transport (7)
Walked or went awkwardly; shuffled (8)
Widows who hold property derived from deceased husbands (8)

Dorian Gray Vocabulary Word Search 2 Answer Key

A very great number of persons or things (6)
Act of watching, especially in secret (6)
An evil, lascivious man; lecher (5)
An inclination to change one's mind impulsively (7)
Anything that relieves distress or pain (7)
Burned superficially or slightly; scorched (6)
Characterized by excessive self-esteem or exaggerated dignity (7)
Cliff with a vertical or overhanging face (9)
Clouded; opaque; obscured (6)
Contemptuously rude or impertinent behavior or speech (10)
Criticize or reproach harshly (7)
Devotion to pleasure as a way of life (8)
Feeling of contempt for anything regarded as unworthy (7)
Feeling of utter weariness and discontent resulting from satiety or lack of interest; boredom (5)
Filthy or dirty; foul (6)
Foolishness (7)
Gruesome; horrible; revolting (5)
Having a gaunt, wasted, or exhausted appearance, as from prolonged suffering, exertion, or anxiety
Having an offensive odor; stinking (5)
Imitate for purposes of ridicule or satire (6)

Landing place constructed along the edge of a body of water (4)
Long, loose, heavy overcoat (6)
Ornamental bands or borders, esp. on ecclesiastical vestments (8)
People who rouse or drive game from cover (7)
Self-righteous person who demands pointless conformity (4)
Set forth or state in detail (7)
Settled securely or snugly (9)
Simple descriptive or narrative piece in verse or prose (5)
Stop developing, growing, or progressing (8)
Strike down, injure, or slay (5)
Talk excessively and pointlessly; babble (5)
To ask (a person) earnestly; beseech; implore (7)
To bring about, produce, or cause (6)
Two-wheeled covered carriage with the driver's seat above and behind (6)
Undesirable conditions or disorders (8)
Various plants of the lily family (8)
Vehicle carrying many passengers, used for public transport (7)
Walked or went awkwardly; shuffled (8)
Widows who hold property derived from deceased husbands (8)

Dorian Gray Vocabulary Word Search 3

```
U N A D U L T E R A T E D C A P R I C E
E T P E I D H V X H T U O C N U G R R P
D U R W M S S I P T H G G G A R D R I W
A R O A Y E D T S O O X W D C P R E Y Q
R B T F R C Y A R P M U T D A D X T G Z
T I E F I N T R I R O Y N R R P A R E H
S D G U A E I O W N Y R O D I Y N I N M
U S E G D L S B E V V D T U T V N E A Q
L U R I D O O O N Y Y T W I S R I V P M
A N Q F I S I R N T G K R M C L H A Y I
B H C Y D N N R U I F C B P K O I B L S
B Y A M R I U O I N O G B A B S L L Z A
V Y S N O E C C F I X M S S B N A E G N
V U T B S D E L D F J L M M O N T D Y T
D V L P E O P E P F T S I I V Y E E Y H
E P I G R A M Q U A Y K T V U L S T E R
X A N P A N I T R E T A E E E O M S E O
L I F B E R E N R P D H M M L R S V F P
S N V T L N I H E A R A O A I Z I F I E
R F A L Y S P T R R L I T S C V R E A L
K R Y D H R U G Y A T E G F A Z O T S M
P D O E O L E K I D S C V M L F J H I C
I N D H A D X I F O L L I E S Q P D O W
A B E N T R E A T L X S S R E G A W O D
Z Z T W Z S N W B S T C E N S U R E R S
```

AFFINITY	ESPIAL	LURID	PROTEGE
ANNIHILATES	EXPOUND	MALADIES	QUAY
ANODYNE	FACILE	MEDIOCRITY	REVIVALIST
APHORISMS	FETID	MISANTHROPE	SATYR
BALUSTRADE	FIASCO	MYRIAD	SINGED
CAPRICE	FOLLIES	ORPHREYS	SMITE
CENSURE	GUFFAWED	PANEGYRIC	SORDID
CORROBORATIVE	HAGGARD	PARASOLS	TARNISHED
DEGRADATION	HANSOM	PARODY	TAWDRY
DESOLATE	IDYLL	PATHOS	TRIVIAL
DISDAIN	IMPASSIVE	PETULANT	TURBID
DOWAGERS	IMPECUNIOSITY	POMPOUS	ULSTER
ENNUI	INSOLENCES	PORTICO	UNADULTERATED
ENTREAT	IRRETRIEVABLE	PRATE	UNCOUTH
EPIGRAM	LIVERIES	PRIG	VULGARITY

Dorian Gray Vocabulary Word Search 3 Answer Key

AFFINITY	ESPIAL	LURID	PROTEGE
ANNIHILATES	EXPOUND	MALADIES	QUAY
ANODYNE	FACILE	MEDIOCRITY	REVIVALIST
APHORISMS	FETID	MISANTHROPE	SATYR
BALUSTRADE	FIASCO	MYRIAD	SINGED
CAPRICE	FOLLIES	ORPHREYS	SMITE
CENSURE	GUFFAWED	PANEGYRIC	SORDID
CORROBORATIVE	HAGGARD	PARASOLS	TARNISHED
DEGRADATION	HANSOM	PARODY	TAWDRY
DESOLATE	IDYLL	PATHOS	TRIVIAL
DISDAIN	IMPASSIVE	PETULANT	TURBID
DOWAGERS	IMPECUNIOSITY	POMPOUS	ULSTER
ENNUI	INSOLENCES	PORTICO	UNADULTERATED
ENTREAT	IRRETRIEVABLE	PRATE	UNCOUTH
EPIGRAM	LIVERIES	PRIG	VULGARITY

Dorian Gray Vocabulary Word Search 4

```
U N C O U T H E E P O R H T N A S I M
E N Y R B T G C P A E D R N O T M N G
X R A D U Q N U I N D R I E U S C S
P E T D L C Q D G E D N V M I R A H
O T N O D I E N R G I U E T B R N G
U A S S U G B I A Y O O I N D I O N D
N E F R C T A L M R U F A O A D H A D
D R P E I O H B E I S Z L T R F P T R
F T C S T X N A R D C S R W A G G A I V
O N Q C M I K C N A I D M P R E O I O L
L E M A L D I E S T C K I B D M V N R
L T T E F I E U G D O E A L T P N N D F
I A N R R I W N E X K M D T E E I G V
E N A U C N A N T L R L Y C E V B V P D
S G L S X V F E O S A M U N L A U U Q B
K A U N K A F R R I A N O N N S L H J
Y T T E M R U Q P F I C G U Q P M G B C
E S E C P I G S N O I M S U D P A R N
P N P L D A E I S T Y T W C I L Q R W
R W T P I B R I R F R Q K C A D S I C L
A B G H D L T O I A I U C H M P L T K H
T A W D R Y P Q D E B A U C H E R Y E N
E W R H O A X E Y Y L Y S J K X S I N F
R Y T A S N L Z L F A C I L E V C M R
P R I G V B W L L A L O D N O G M X Y E
```

ABDICATE
APHORISMS
ATONEMENT
BALUSTRADE
BRACKEN
CAPRICE
CENSURE
CRUCIBLE
DEBAUCHERY
DEGRADATION
DESOLATE
ENNUI
ENSCONCED
ENTHRALL
ENTREAT

EPIGRAM
ESPIAL
EXPOUND
FACILE
FETID
FIASCO
FLACCID
FOLLIES
FOUNDER
GONDOLA
GUFFAWED
HANSOM
IDYLL
IMPECUNIOSITY
INCARNATION

INDUCE
INFAMY
INVARIABLY
LANGUIDLY
LURID
MALADIES
MISANTHROPE
OMNIBUS
PANEGYRIC
PARODY
PETULANT
PORTICO
PRATE
PRIG
PROTEGE

PRUDENCE
QUAY
SATYR
SINGED
SMITE
SORDID
STAGNATE
TAWDRY
TEDIOUS
TRIVIAL
TURBID
ULSTER
UNADULTERATED
UNCOUTH
VULGARITY

Dorian Gray Vocabulary Word Search 4 Answer Key

ABDICATE	EPIGRAM	INDUCE	PRUDENCE
APHORISMS	ESPIAL	INFAMY	QUAY
ATONEMENT	EXPOUND	INVARIABLY	SATYR
BALUSTRADE	FACILE	LANGUIDLY	SINGED
BRACKEN	FETID	LURID	SMITE
CAPRICE	FIASCO	MALADIES	SORDID
CENSURE	FLACCID	MISANTHROPE	STAGNATE
CRUCIBLE	FOLLIES	OMNIBUS	TAWDRY
DEBAUCHERY	FOUNDER	PANEGYRIC	TEDIOUS
DEGRADATION	GONDOLA	PARODY	TRIVIAL
DESOLATE	GUFFAWED	PETULANT	TURBID
ENNUI	HANSOM	PORTICO	ULSTER
ENSCONCED	IDYLL	PRATE	UNADULTERATED
ENTHRALL	IMPECUNIOSITY	PRIG	UNCOUTH
ENTREAT	INCARNATION	PROTEGE	VULGARITY

Dorian Gray Vocabulary Crossword 1

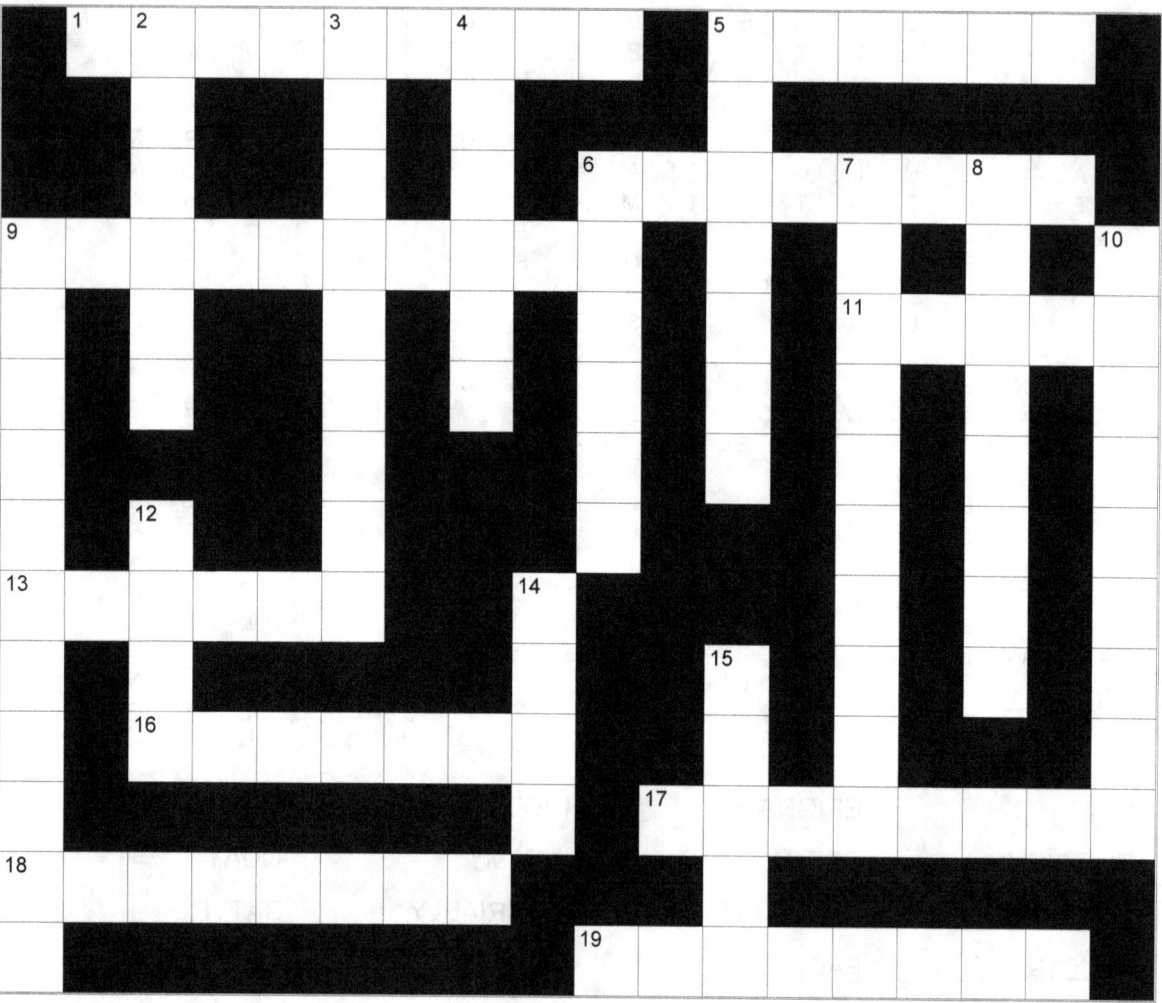

Across
1. Amends or reparation made for an injury or wrong
5. Easily done, performed, or used
6. Undesirable conditions or disorders
9. State of being ordinary; not outstanding
11. An evil, lascivious man; lecher
13. Clouded; opaque; obscured
16. Long narrow flat-bottomed boat propelled by sculling
17. Caution with regard to practical matters; discretion
18. Obtained or gotten by care, effort, or the use of special means
19. Renounce or relinquish a throne, right, or power

Down
2. Gaudy; showy and cheap
3. Settled securely or snugly
4. Act of watching, especially in secret
5. Foolishness
6. A very great number of persons or things
7. Freed from an engagement, pledge, or obligation
8. Captivate or charm
9. Hater of humankind
10. Cliff with a vertical or overhanging face
12. Self-righteous person who demands pointless conformity
14. Landing place constructed along the edge of a body of water
15. Gruesome; horrible; revolting

Dorian Gray Vocabulary Crossword 1 Answer Key

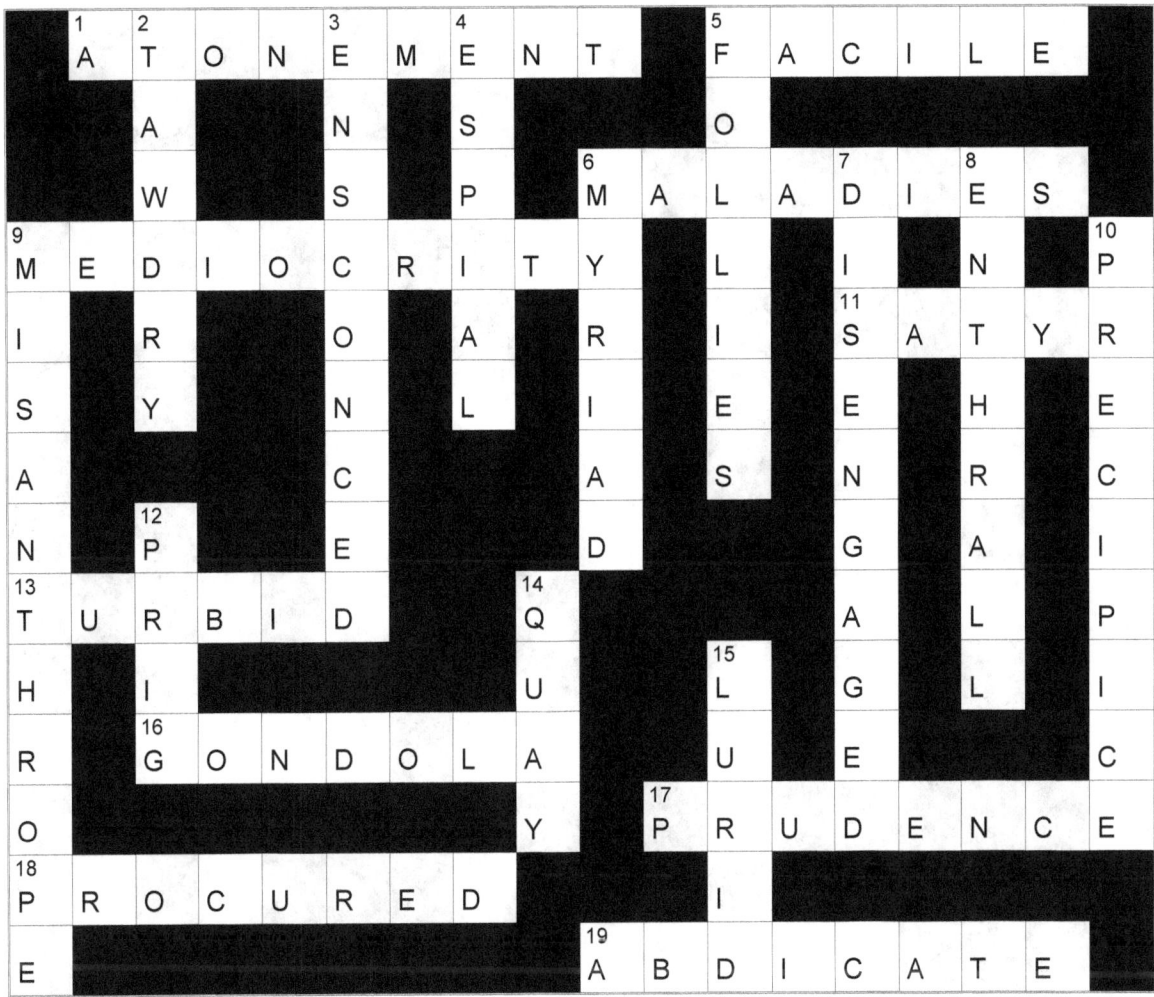

Across
1. Amends or reparation made for an injury or wrong
5. Easily done, performed, or used
6. Undesirable conditions or disorders
9. State of being ordinary; not outstanding
11. An evil, lascivious man; lecher
13. Clouded; opaque; obscured
16. Long narrow flat-bottomed boat propelled by sculling
17. Caution with regard to practical matters; discretion
18. Obtained or gotten by care, effort, or the use of special means
19. Renounce or relinquish a throne, right, or power

Down
2. Gaudy; showy and cheap
3. Settled securely or snugly
4. Act of watching, especially in secret
5. Foolishness
6. A very great number of persons or things
7. Freed from an engagement, pledge, or obligation
8. Captivate or charm
9. Hater of humankind
10. Cliff with a vertical or overhanging face
12. Self-righteous person who demands pointless conformity
14. Landing place constructed along the edge of a body of water
15. Gruesome; horrible; revolting

Dorian Gray Vocabulary Crossword 2

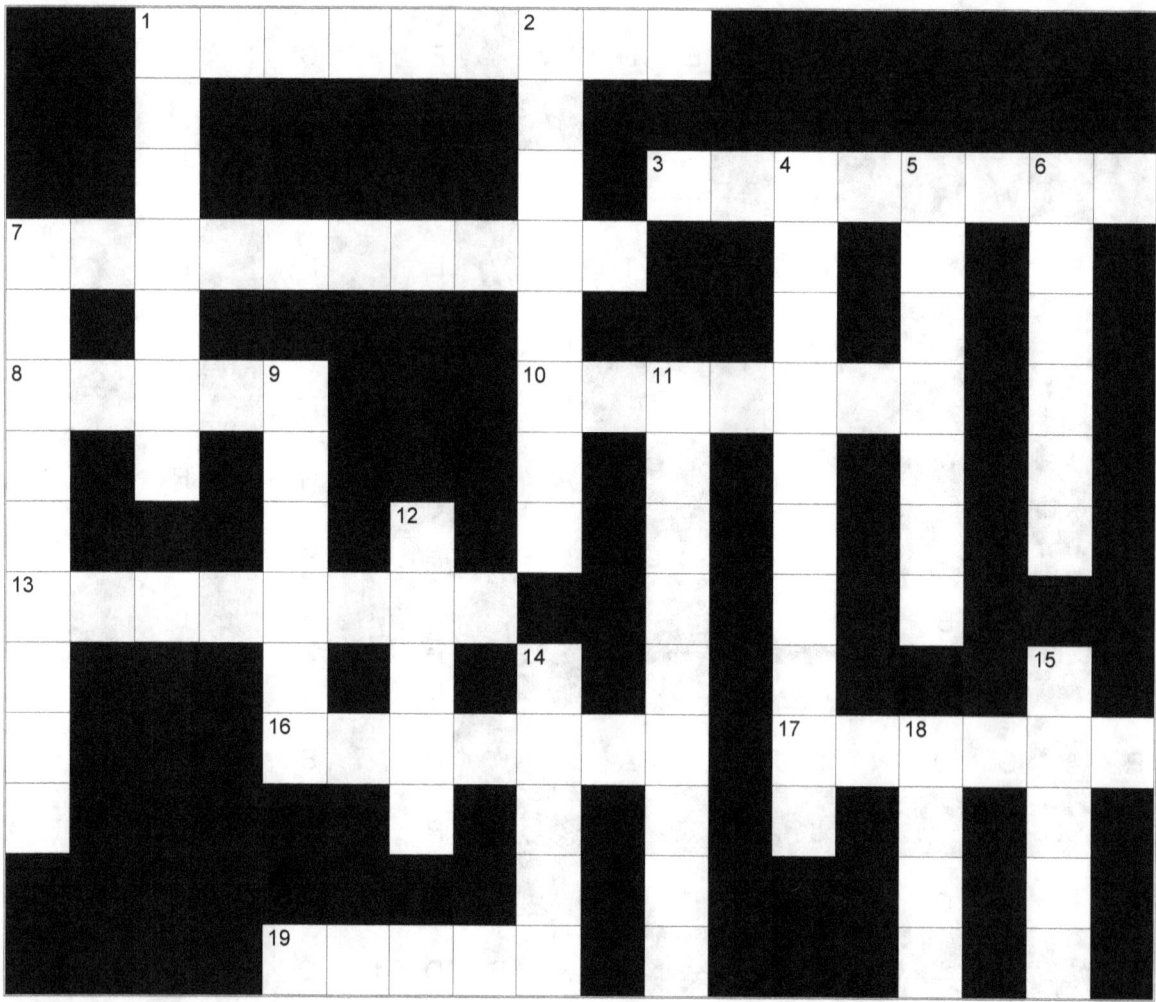

Across
1. Settled securely or snugly
3. Renounce or relinquish a throne, right, or power
7. Reckless extravagance
8. Feeling of utter weariness and discontent resulting from satiety or lack of interest; boredom
10. People who rouse or drive game from cover
13. Obtained or gotten by care, effort, or the use of special means
16. Concise, clever, often paradoxical statement
17. Act of watching, especially in secret
19. Strike down, injure, or slay

Down
1. Set forth or state in detail
2. Severe, searching test or trial
4. Freed from an engagement, pledge, or obligation
5. Criticize or reproach harshly
6. Gaudy; showy and cheap
7. Cliff with a vertical or overhanging face
9. To bring about, produce, or cause
11. Amends or reparation made for an injury or wrong
12. Having an offensive odor; stinking
14. Talk excessively and pointlessly; babble
15. An evil, lascivious man; lecher
18. Self-righteous person who demands pointless conformity

Dorian Gray Vocabulary Crossword 2 Answer Key

Across
1. Settled securely or snugly
3. Renounce or relinquish a throne, right, or power
7. Reckless extravagance
8. Feeling of utter weariness and discontent resulting from satiety or lack of interest; boredom
10. People who rouse or drive game from cover
13. Obtained or gotten by care, effort, or the use of special means
16. Concise, clever, often paradoxical statement
17. Act of watching, especially in secret
19. Strike down, injure, or slay

Down
1. Set forth or state in detail
2. Severe, searching test or trial
4. Freed from an engagement, pledge, or obligation
5. Criticize or reproach harshly
6. Gaudy; showy and cheap
7. Cliff with a vertical or overhanging face
9. To bring about, produce, or cause
11. Amends or reparation made for an injury or wrong
12. Having an offensive odor; stinking
14. Talk excessively and pointlessly; babble
15. An evil, lascivious man; lecher
18. Self-righteous person who demands pointless conformity

Dorian Gray Vocabulary Crossword 3

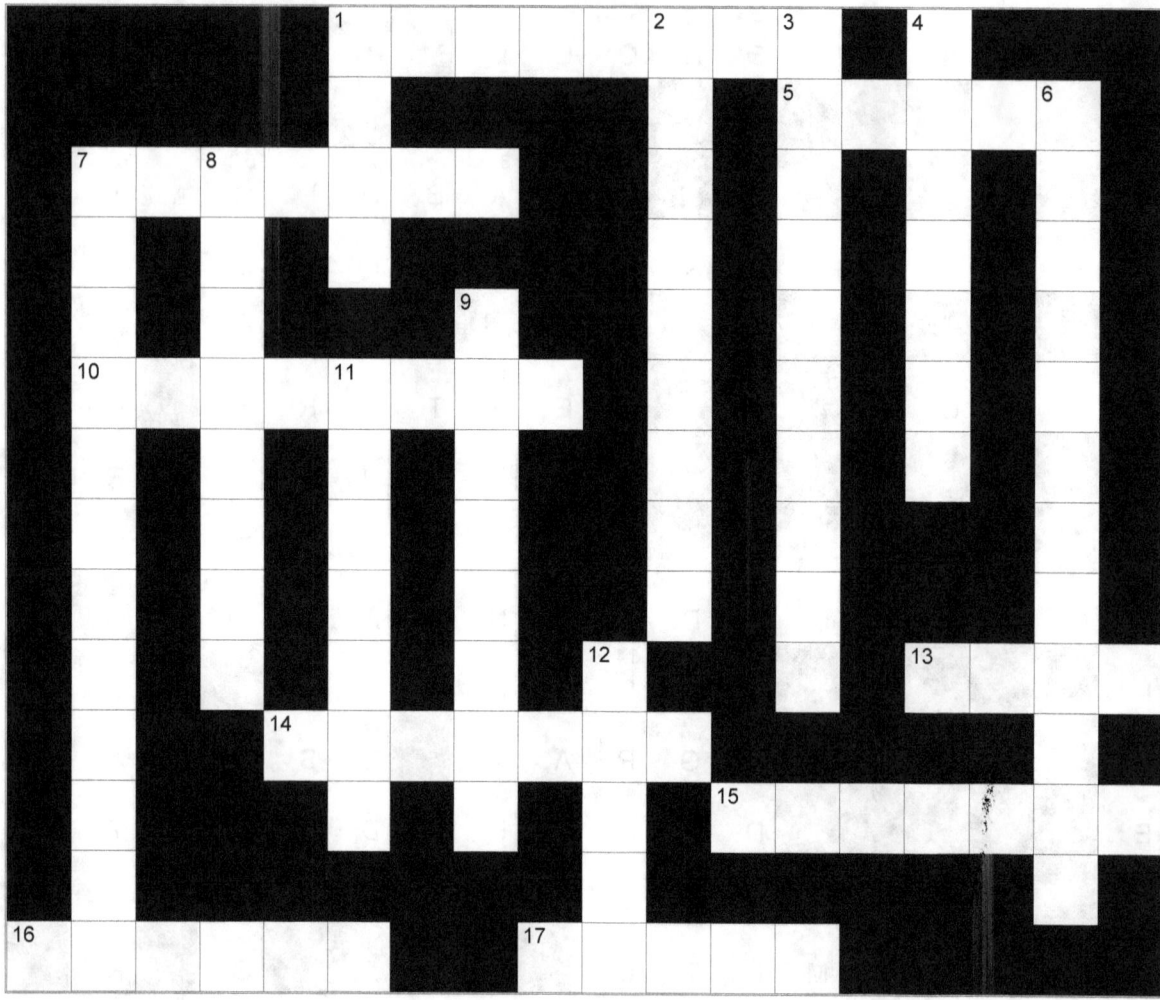

Across
1. Obtained or gotten by care, effort, or the use of special means
5. Feeling of utter weariness and discontent resulting from satiety or lack of interest; boredom
7. An inclination to change one's mind impulsively
10. Walked or went awkwardly; shuffled
13. Landing place constructed along the edge of a body of water
14. Criticize or reproach harshly
15. Long narrow flat-bottomed boat propelled by sculling
16. A very great number of persons or things
17. Having an offensive odor; stinking

Down
1. Self-righteous person who demands pointless conformity
2. Answer to a reply; response
3. Excessive indulgence in sensual pleasures
4. Anything that relieves distress or pain
6. Seeming to be without an end; endless
7. Greenhouse, usually attached to a dwelling
8. Light, usually small umbrellas carried as protection from the sun
9. Devotion to pleasure as a way of life
11. Area overgrown with ferns and shrubs
12. Talk excessively and pointlessly; babble

Dorian Gray Vocabulary Crossword 3 Answer Key

Across
1. Obtained or gotten by care, effort, or the use of special means
5. Feeling of utter weariness and discontent resulting from satiety or lack of interest; boredom
7. An inclination to change one's mind impulsively
10. Walked or went awkwardly; shuffled
13. Landing place constructed along the edge of a body of water
14. Criticize or reproach harshly
15. Long narrow flat-bottomed boat propelled by sculling
16. A very great number of persons or things
17. Having an offensive odor; stinking

Down
1. Self-righteous person who demands pointless conformity
2. Answer to a reply; response
3. Excessive indulgence in sensual pleasures
4. Anything that relieves distress or pain
6. Seeming to be without an end; endless
7. Greenhouse, usually attached to a dwelling
8. Light, usually small umbrellas carried as protection from the sun
9. Devotion to pleasure as a way of life
11. Area overgrown with ferns and shrubs
12. Talk excessively and pointlessly; babble

Dorian Gray Vocabulary Crossword 4

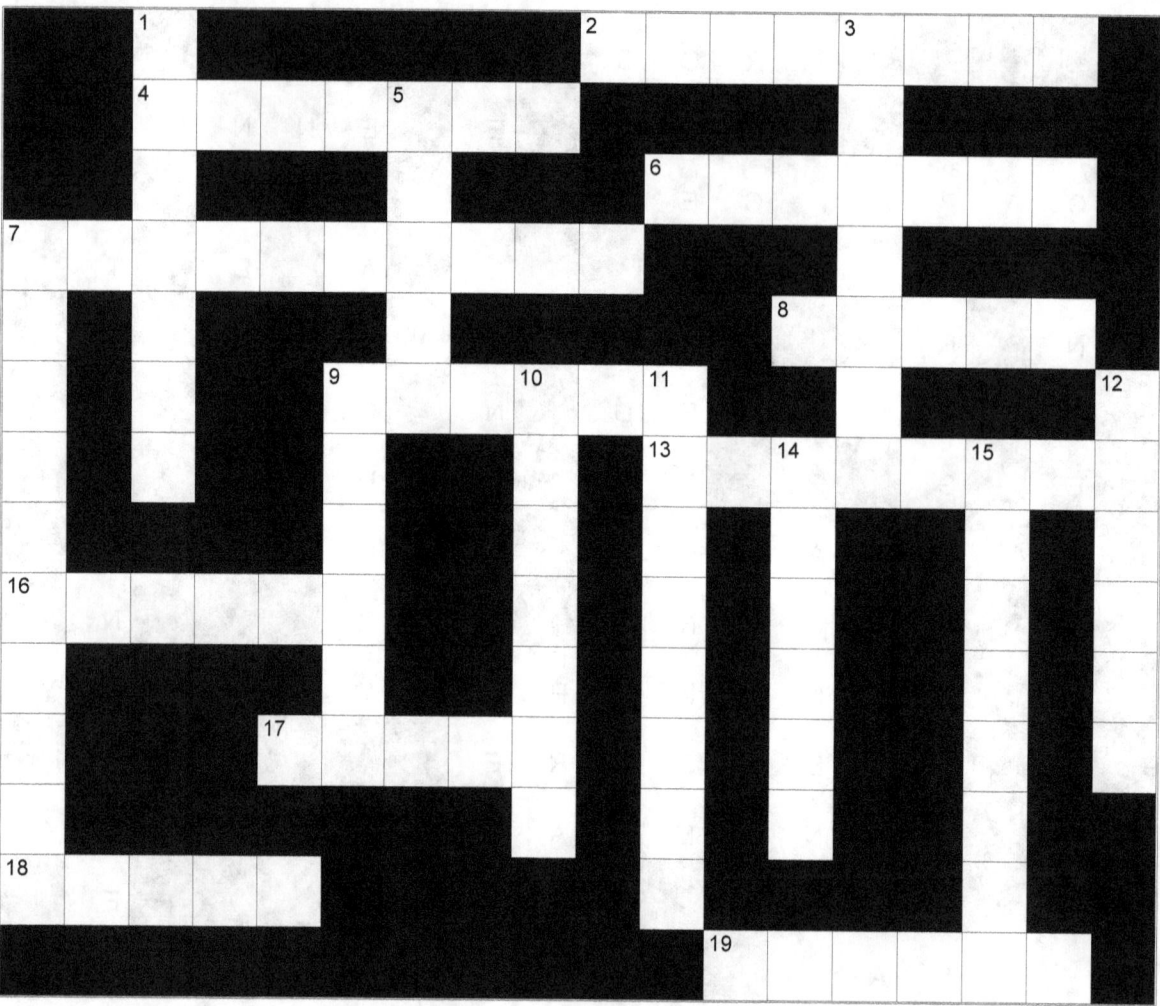

Across
2. Cheerfully optimistic, hopeful, or confident
4. To ask (a person) earnestly; beseech; implore
6. Soft and limp; not firm; flabby
7. Contemptuously rude or impertinent behavior or speech
8. Gruesome; horrible; revolting
9. Burned superficially or slightly; scorched
13. Captivate or charm
16. Clouded; opaque; obscured
17. Simple descriptive or narrative piece in verse or prose
18. An evil, lascivious man; lecher
19. Easily done, performed, or used

Down
1. Criticize or reproach harshly
3. Awkward, clumsy, or unmannerly
5. Feeling of utter weariness and discontent resulting from satiety or lack of interest; boredom
7. Having excessive or blind adoration, reverence, or devotion
9. Filthy or dirty; foul
10. Long narrow flat-bottomed boat propelled by sculling
11. Feeling abandoned; forlorn
12. Long, loose, heavy overcoat
14. Gaudy; showy and cheap
15. Various plants of the lily family

Dorian Gray Vocabulary Crossword 4 Answer Key

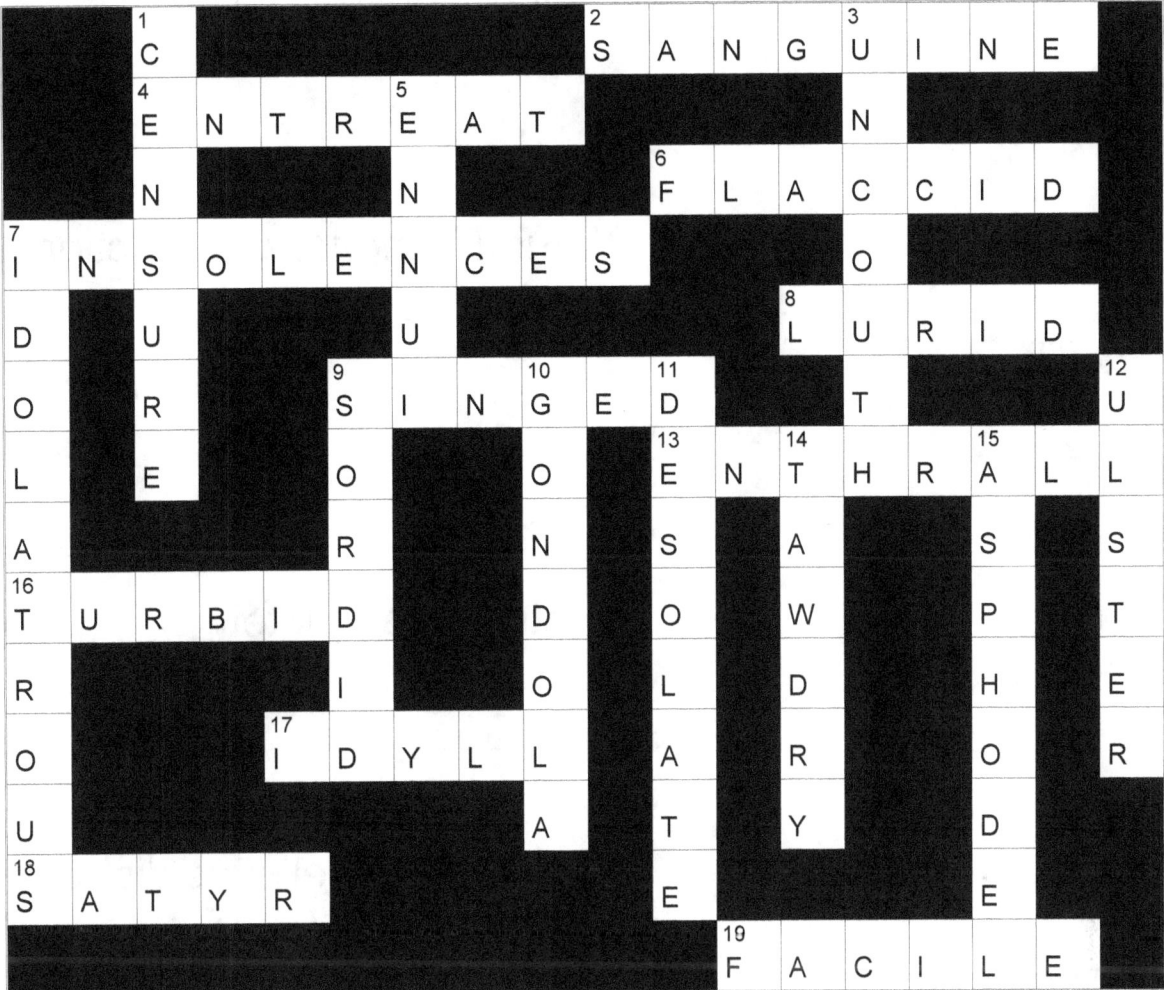

Across
2. Cheerfully optimistic, hopeful, or confident
4. To ask (a person) earnestly; beseech; implore
6. Soft and limp; not firm; flabby
7. Contemptuously rude or impertinent behavior or speech
8. Gruesome; horrible; revolting
9. Burned superficially or slightly; scorched
13. Captivate or charm
16. Clouded; opaque; obscured
17. Simple descriptive or narrative piece in verse or prose
18. An evil, lascivious man; lecher
19. Easily done, performed, or used

Down
1. Criticize or reproach harshly
3. Awkward, clumsy, or unmannerly
5. Feeling of utter weariness and discontent resulting from satiety or lack of interest; boredom
7. Having excessive or blind adoration, reverence, or devotion
9. Filthy or dirty; foul
10. Long narrow flat-bottomed boat propelled by sculling
11. Feeling abandoned; forlorn
12. Long, loose, heavy overcoat
14. Gaudy; showy and cheap
15. Various plants of the lily family

ABDICATE	Renounce or relinquish a throne, right, or power
AFFINITY	Natural liking for or attraction to a person, thing, idea, etc.
ANNIHILATES	Destroys completely
ANODYNE	Anything that relieves distress or pain
APHORISMS	Tersely phrased statements of truth or opinion; adages
ASPHODEL	Various plants of the lily family

ATONEMENT	Amends or reparation made for an injury or wrong
BALUSTRADE	Railing at the side of a staircase or balcony
BEATERS	People who rouse or drive game from cover
BRACKEN	Area overgrown with ferns and shrubs
BROUGHAM	Closed four-wheeled carriage with an open driver's seat in the front
CAPRICE	An inclination to change one's mind impulsively

CENSURE	Criticize or reproach harshly
CONJECTURES	Judgments based on inconclusive or incomplete evidence
CONSERVATORY	Greenhouse, usually attached to a dwelling
CORROBORATIVE	Serving to support or to make more certain
CRUCIBLE	Severe, searching test or trial
DEBAUCHERY	Excessive indulgence in sensual pleasures

DEGRADATION	A decline to a lower condition, quality, or level
DESOLATE	Feeling abandoned; forlorn
DISDAIN	Feeling of contempt for anything regarded as unworthy
DISENGAGED	Freed from an engagement, pledge, or obligation
DOWAGERS	Widows who hold property derived from deceased husbands
ELOCUTION	Person's manner of speaking or reading aloud in public

ENNUI	Feeling of utter weariness and discontent resulting from satiety or lack of interest; boredom
ENSCONCED	Settled securely or snugly
ENTHRALL	Captivate or charm
ENTREAT	To ask (a person) earnestly; beseech; implore
EPIGRAM	Concise, clever, often paradoxical statement
ESPIAL	Act of watching, especially in secret

EXPOUND	Set forth or state in detail
FACILE	Easily done, performed, or used
FETID	Having an offensive odor; stinking
FIASCO	Complete and humiliting failure
FLACCID	Soft and limp; not firm; flabby
FOLLIES	Foolishness

FOUNDER	Fill with water and sink
GONDOLA	Long narrow flat-bottomed boat propelled by sculling
GUFFAWED	Laughed heartily and boisterously
HAGGARD	Having a gaunt, wasted, or exhausted appearance, as from prolonged suffering, exertion, or anxiety
HANSOM	Two-wheeled covered carriage with the driver's seat above and behind
HEDONISM	Devotion to pleasure as a way of life

IDOLATROUS	Having excessive or blind adoration, reverence, or devotion
IDYLL	Simple descriptive or narrative piece in verse or prose
IMPASSIVE	Without emotion; apathetic; unmoved
IMPECUNIOSITY	State of having little or no money; penniless; poor
INCARNATION	Assumption of human form or nature
INCORRIGIBLE	Difficult or impossible to control or manage

INDUCE	To bring about, produce, or cause
INFAMY	Extremly bad reputation
INSOLENCES	Contemptuously rude or impertinent behavior or speech
INTERMINABLE	Seeming to be without an end; endless
INVARIABLY	Without variation or change, in every case
IRRETRIEVABLE	Unable to be recovered or regained

LANGUIDLY	In a manner lacking in spirit or interest; listlessly; indifferently
LIVERIES	Uniforms worn by servants
LUCRATIVE	Producing wealth; profitable
LURID	Gruesome; horrible; revolting
MALADIES	Undesirable conditions or disorders
MEDIOCRITY	State of being ordinary; not outstanding

MISANTHROPE	Hater of humankind
MYRIAD	A very great number of persons or things
OMNIBUS	Vehicle carrying many passengers, used for public transport
ORPHREYS	Ornamental bands or borders, esp. on ecclesiastical vestments
PANEGYRIC	Formal or elaborate praise
PARASOLS	Light, usually small umbrellas carried as protection from the sun

PARODY	Imitate for purposes of ridicule or satire
PATHOS	Feeling of sympathy or pity
PETULANT	Unreasonably irritable or ill-tempered
PHILANTHROPY	Effort or inclination to increase the well-being of humankind
POMPOUS	Characterized by excessive self-esteem or exaggerated dignity
PORTICO	Structure consisting of a roof supported by columns or piers, usually attached to a building

PRATE	Talk excessively and pointlessly; babble
PRECIPICE	Cliff with a vertical or overhanging face
PRESENTIMENT	Feeling of evil to come
PRIG	Self-righteous person who demands pointless conformity
PROCURED	Obtained or gotten by care, effort, or the use of special means
PROFLIGACY	Reckless extravagance

PROTEGE	One whose welfare is promoted by an influential person
PRUDENCE	Caution with regard to practical matters; discretion
QUAY	Landing place constructed along the edge of a body of water
REJOINDER	Answer to a reply; response
REVIVALIST	Person who promotes or holds religious revivals
SANGUINE	Cheerfully optimistic, hopeful, or confident

SATYR	An evil, lascivious man; lecher
SHAMBLED	Walked or went awkwardly; shuffled
SINGED	Burned superficially or slightly; scorched
SMITE	Strike down, injure, or slay
SORDID	Filthy or dirty; foul
STAGNATE	Stop developing, growing, or progressing

TARNISHED	Diminished or became tainted
TAWDRY	Gaudy; showy and cheap
TEDIOUS	Boring, tiring, monotonous, dull
TRIVIAL	Of very little importance or value; insignificant
TURBID	Clouded; opaque; obscured
ULSTER	Long, loose, heavy overcoat

UNADULTERATED	Not mixed with impurities; without qualification
UNCOUTH	Awkward, clumsy, or unmannerly
VULGARITY	Act or expression that offends good taste or propriety
WAINSCOTING	Wood paneling for lining interior walls

Dorian Gray Vocabulary

PARASOLS	APHORISMS	CONSERVATORY	STAGNATE	PROTEGE
TARNISHED	FOLLIES	LIVERIES	MEDIOCRITY	ENTREAT
PETULANT	PATHOS	FREE SPACE	CENSURE	ORPHREYS
VULGARITY	UNADULTERATED	BRACKEN	ASPHODEL	REVIVALIST
MYRIAD	TAWDRY	SMITE	ANODYNE	WAINSCOTING

Dorian Gray Vocabulary

INCARNATION	TRIVIAL	SORDID	LUCRATIVE	DISENGAGED
TURBID	LANGUIDLY	REJOINDER	INCORRIGIBLE	FOUNDER
HEDONISM	POMPOUS	FREE SPACE	QUAY	ENNUI
ATONEMENT	PORTICO	CONJECTURES	BEATERS	INSOLENCES
BROUGHAM	SATYR	CAPRICE	PROCURED	SANGUINE

Dorian Gray Vocabulary

LUCRATIVE	PRESENTIMENT	VULGARITY	ENNUI	CONJECTURES
PRUDENCE	GUFFAWED	STAGNATE	LURID	ENTHRALL
FLACCID	PROFLIGACY	FREE SPACE	ESPIAL	BROUGHAM
ENSCONCED	BEATERS	QUAY	TRIVIAL	FETID
OMNIBUS	PATHOS	INCORRIGIBLE	ATONEMENT	UNADULTERATED

Dorian Gray Vocabulary

ULSTER	TURBID	PROTEGE	INTERMINABLE	IRRETRIEVABLE
HEDONISM	PETULANT	ABDICATE	DOWAGERS	IMPASSIVE
SANGUINE	PHILANTHROPY	FREE SPACE	LANGUIDLY	INSOLENCES
WAINSCOTING	DISENGAGED	FACILE	PANEGYRIC	SHAMBLED
LIVERIES	IMPECUNIOSITY	ORPHREYS	APHORISMS	REVIVALIST

Dorian Gray Vocabulary

CONJECTURES	PARODY	AFFINITY	SORDID	WAINSCOTING
TURBID	DISDAIN	INSOLENCES	ANNIHILATES	STAGNATE
INTERMINABLE	QUAY	FREE SPACE	INCORRIGIBLE	GONDOLA
INFAMY	PRUDENCE	BEATERS	ATONEMENT	FLACCID
IDOLATROUS	CAPRICE	EPIGRAM	ELOCUTION	DOWAGERS

Dorian Gray Vocabulary

CRUCIBLE	SMITE	LURID	ENNUI	POMPOUS
MEDIOCRITY	OMNIBUS	DISENGAGED	FOLLIES	PARASOLS
INVARIABLY	ASPHODEL	FREE SPACE	DEGRADATION	MISANTHROPE
ENTREAT	ESPIAL	TARNISHED	INCARNATION	ULSTER
PRECIPICE	CONSERVATORY	HEDONISM	TEDIOUS	HAGGARD

Dorian Gray Vocabulary

FIASCO	PRECIPICE	DESOLATE	MYRIAD	PROCURED
INFAMY	HEDONISM	PROTEGE	DISDAIN	ULSTER
ESPIAL	BROUGHAM	FREE SPACE	CAPRICE	SHAMBLED
PATHOS	FOUNDER	INVARIABLY	TARNISHED	UNADULTERATED
ENNUI	INTERMINABLE	INCORRIGIBLE	APHORISMS	SANGUINE

Dorian Gray Vocabulary

BEATERS	LURID	DEGRADATION	LIVERIES	PHILANTHROPY
MISANTHROPE	INCARNATION	OMNIBUS	IDYLL	EPIGRAM
POMPOUS	FACILE	FREE SPACE	BRACKEN	CORROBORATIVE
PRESENTIMENT	STAGNATE	ENSCONCED	CENSURE	INDUCE
BALUSTRADE	VULGARITY	ANNIHILATES	PETULANT	ORPHREYS

Dorian Gray Vocabulary

FETID	DISENGAGED	LURID	PARODY	PRIG
UNADULTERATED	OMNIBUS	PETULANT	APHORISMS	VULGARITY
MYRIAD	SORDID	FREE SPACE	CONJECTURES	STAGNATE
WAINSCOTING	BALUSTRADE	REJOINDER	ANNIHILATES	TEDIOUS
CENSURE	DEGRADATION	EPIGRAM	EXPOUND	MALADIES

Dorian Gray Vocabulary

PROCURED	INCORRIGIBLE	TURBID	FOUNDER	PATHOS
ANODYNE	SATYR	ELOCUTION	FOLLIES	HEDONISM
FIASCO	AFFINITY	FREE SPACE	CORROBORATIVE	MEDIOCRITY
DOWAGERS	INVARIABLY	PRATE	BEATERS	PORTICO
ENTREAT	PRUDENCE	TARNISHED	PARASOLS	ULSTER

Dorian Gray Vocabulary

CAPRICE	POMPOUS	DESOLATE	MEDIOCRITY	ABDICATE
INCORRIGIBLE	ELOCUTION	PETULANT	ENSCONCED	LURID
ANODYNE	EXPOUND	FREE SPACE	FETID	SATYR
DEGRADATION	PARODY	FIASCO	PANEGYRIC	DISENGAGED
IRRETRIEVABLE	LUCRATIVE	HEDONISM	CONSERVATORY	SMITE

Dorian Gray Vocabulary

PROFLIGACY	IDOLATROUS	QUAY	SANGUINE	MISANTHROPE
ASPHODEL	INFAMY	CENSURE	IMPECUNIOSITY	ESPIAL
ENTREAT	PROCURED	FREE SPACE	PHILANTHROPY	SINGED
DISDAIN	CORROBORATIVE	UNADULTERATED	MALADIES	ANNIHILATES
FACILE	REVIVALIST	TAWDRY	DOWAGERS	AFFINITY

Dorian Gray Vocabulary

SATYR	TEDIOUS	HEDONISM	INVARIABLY	PROTEGE
INDUCE	DOWAGERS	REJOINDER	LANGUIDLY	INCARNATION
VULGARITY	DISENGAGED	FREE SPACE	REVIVALIST	PRECIPICE
PRIG	SHAMBLED	SORDID	PARASOLS	ULSTER
GUFFAWED	ENSCONCED	DESOLATE	MALADIES	SMITE

Dorian Gray Vocabulary

TARNISHED	PORTICO	CORROBORATIVE	UNCOUTH	ANNIHILATES
PROFLIGACY	LURID	CONJECTURES	FLACCID	TRIVIAL
EXPOUND	ENNUI	FREE SPACE	IDOLATROUS	INTERMINABLE
CRUCIBLE	BROUGHAM	PHILANTHROPY	PROCURED	ATONEMENT
PATHOS	IMPECUNIOSITY	ABDICATE	BEATERS	ASPHODEL

Dorian Gray Vocabulary

SMITE	INVARIABLY	PORTICO	TAWDRY	ENTREAT
TARNISHED	PRECIPICE	DEBAUCHERY	EXPOUND	PRESENTIMENT
CAPRICE	INFAMY	FREE SPACE	TEDIOUS	INCARNATION
REJOINDER	ORPHREYS	SORDID	IMPASSIVE	IMPECUNIOSITY
PETULANT	QUAY	HANSOM	CENSURE	ENNUI

Dorian Gray Vocabulary

FOUNDER	CONJECTURES	FOLLIES	REVIVALIST	ESPIAL
BALUSTRADE	LURID	INDUCE	DISDAIN	HAGGARD
PANEGYRIC	POMPOUS	FREE SPACE	INSOLENCES	ANNIHILATES
PRUDENCE	EPIGRAM	LUCRATIVE	PROCURED	MISANTHROPE
WAINSCOTING	ENTHRALL	DOWAGERS	GONDOLA	VULGARITY

Dorian Gray Vocabulary

UNCOUTH	PANEGYRIC	EPIGRAM	PRESENTIMENT	REVIVALIST
INCORRIGIBLE	FIASCO	POMPOUS	DESOLATE	PETULANT
SHAMBLED	PRATE	FREE SPACE	IDYLL	HANSOM
INSOLENCES	PORTICO	FOUNDER	INTERMINABLE	SMITE
STAGNATE	ANNIHILATES	IRRETRIEVABLE	MISANTHROPE	SORDID

Dorian Gray Vocabulary

BRACKEN	INCARNATION	EXPOUND	GUFFAWED	ENTHRALL
AFFINITY	TEDIOUS	ANODYNE	CONJECTURES	FACILE
HEDONISM	PRECIPICE	FREE SPACE	OMNIBUS	TRIVIAL
ENSCONCED	LURID	FETID	INVARIABLY	PRUDENCE
DISDAIN	TARNISHED	APHORISMS	PRIG	FOLLIES

Dorian Gray Vocabulary

INSOLENCES	QUAY	FIASCO	SINGED	CRUCIBLE
SMITE	HAGGARD	IDYLL	IDOLATROUS	FLACCID
INFAMY	TARNISHED	FREE SPACE	ULSTER	APHORISMS
PARODY	INDUCE	PORTICO	EPIGRAM	LANGUIDLY
ENTREAT	DISENGAGED	BALUSTRADE	TURBID	REJOINDER

Dorian Gray Vocabulary

ENNUI	PROCURED	FACILE	BEATERS	FOUNDER
ANODYNE	STAGNATE	INTERMINABLE	WAINSCOTING	GUFFAWED
BROUGHAM	LUCRATIVE	FREE SPACE	DEGRADATION	PATHOS
OMNIBUS	ANNIHILATES	EXPOUND	FOLLIES	MALADIES
CONSERVATORY	PRUDENCE	DEBAUCHERY	SHAMBLED	PRESENTIMENT

Dorian Gray Vocabulary

ESPIAL	VULGARITY	LUCRATIVE	CENSURE	AFFINITY
ANNIHILATES	TRIVIAL	TEDIOUS	WAINSCOTING	SHAMBLED
MALADIES	TAWDRY	FREE SPACE	DISDAIN	EPIGRAM
PATHOS	ELOCUTION	TURBID	FOUNDER	LIVERIES
FLACCID	PRUDENCE	CAPRICE	PRESENTIMENT	SORDID

Dorian Gray Vocabulary

ANODYNE	SMITE	ASPHODEL	PROCURED	OMNIBUS
PANEGYRIC	LANGUIDLY	DISENGAGED	HEDONISM	PORTICO
POMPOUS	SINGED	FREE SPACE	INCARNATION	INCORRIGIBLE
INFAMY	ENTREAT	FIASCO	PROTEGE	ATONEMENT
ENNUI	PRIG	CONJECTURES	GONDOLA	GUFFAWED

Dorian Gray Vocabulary

IMPECUNIOSITY	INCORRIGIBLE	PATHOS	WAINSCOTING	EPIGRAM
REVIVALIST	CENSURE	DEBAUCHERY	DISENGAGED	DOWAGERS
INFAMY	PARASOLS	FREE SPACE	PANEGYRIC	LANGUIDLY
ULSTER	INCARNATION	QUAY	ELOCUTION	ENSCONCED
TAWDRY	ENTHRALL	LURID	ENTREAT	BALUSTRADE

Dorian Gray Vocabulary

SINGED	FOUNDER	FOLLIES	STAGNATE	TARNISHED
DEGRADATION	ENNUI	HANSOM	MEDIOCRITY	CORROBORATIVE
UNADULTERATED	VULGARITY	FREE SPACE	LIVERIES	PHILANTHROPY
DESOLATE	IDOLATROUS	SHAMBLED	PRECIPICE	ATONEMENT
HAGGARD	PORTICO	APHORISMS	SATYR	FIASCO

Dorian Gray Vocabulary

IMPASSIVE	FOUNDER	MYRIAD	FACILE	FOLLIES
ENNUI	INTERMINABLE	EXPOUND	ESPIAL	LURID
PRECIPICE	TAWDRY	FREE SPACE	SANGUINE	ANNIHILATES
PRATE	DEBAUCHERY	PORTICO	IMPECUNIOSITY	GONDOLA
IDOLATROUS	PETULANT	LUCRATIVE	MALADIES	OMNIBUS

Dorian Gray Vocabulary

CENSURE	LANGUIDLY	DEGRADATION	TURBID	LIVERIES
IDYLL	PRUDENCE	APHORISMS	VULGARITY	INCORRIGIBLE
INVARIABLY	PROTEGE	FREE SPACE	ABDICATE	FLACCID
HANSOM	INSOLENCES	MEDIOCRITY	SINGED	CORROBORATIVE
IRRETRIEVABLE	FIASCO	ANODYNE	UNADULTERATED	INCARNATION

Dorian Gray Vocabulary

MYRIAD	GUFFAWED	ANNIHILATES	LUCRATIVE	FLACCID
PANEGYRIC	CONJECTURES	POMPOUS	DEBAUCHERY	EXPOUND
INCORRIGIBLE	PETULANT	FREE SPACE	LANGUIDLY	DESOLATE
EPIGRAM	DEGRADATION	PHILANTHROPY	PRATE	VULGARITY
ATONEMENT	PRIG	FETID	ENTREAT	REJOINDER

Dorian Gray Vocabulary

SHAMBLED	MALADIES	IMPASSIVE	PARODY	BRACKEN
ENNUI	TARNISHED	BEATERS	BROUGHAM	FIASCO
INSOLENCES	ESPIAL	FREE SPACE	PRUDENCE	LURID
INVARIABLY	PRECIPICE	HAGGARD	ABDICATE	STAGNATE
FACILE	IDOLATROUS	UNADULTERATED	IMPECUNIOSITY	DISDAIN

Dorian Gray Vocabulary

TARNISHED	TURBID	POMPOUS	PARODY	BEATERS
FLACCID	TEDIOUS	FOUNDER	PROFLIGACY	LIVERIES
PRUDENCE	PETULANT	FREE SPACE	VULGARITY	STAGNATE
PATHOS	PORTICO	CAPRICE	ANODYNE	ABDICATE
CRUCIBLE	ORPHREYS	PROTEGE	FACILE	INCARNATION

Dorian Gray Vocabulary

AFFINITY	UNCOUTH	IMPASSIVE	LANGUIDLY	IMPECUNIOSITY
ENTREAT	HAGGARD	MEDIOCRITY	HEDONISM	LUCRATIVE
ASPHODEL	ANNIHILATES	FREE SPACE	APHORISMS	WAINSCOTING
OMNIBUS	DISENGAGED	IDOLATROUS	EXPOUND	DISDAIN
CORROBORATIVE	BALUSTRADE	GONDOLA	CONJECTURES	SHAMBLED

Dorian Gray Vocabulary

PRIG	ESPIAL	ENTREAT	TAWDRY	BRACKEN
DISENGAGED	SMITE	IMPASSIVE	INFAMY	MALADIES
FIASCO	ANNIHILATES	FREE SPACE	HAGGARD	CONSERVATORY
ASPHODEL	OMNIBUS	ELOCUTION	ANODYNE	SATYR
MISANTHROPE	REJOINDER	TARNISHED	CRUCIBLE	ULSTER

Dorian Gray Vocabulary

ENSCONCED	CENSURE	PRUDENCE	WAINSCOTING	APHORISMS
HANSOM	FLACCID	CAPRICE	PETULANT	GONDOLA
PHILANTHROPY	FOUNDER	FREE SPACE	DESOLATE	IRRETRIEVABLE
ORPHREYS	SORDID	VULGARITY	PROFLIGACY	PRATE
FOLLIES	ATONEMENT	PORTICO	CONJECTURES	PROCURED

www.ingramcontent.com/pod-product-compliance
Lightning Source LLC
Chambersburg PA
CBHW081450070526
44586CB00019B/2292